EUDES PICARD'S
TAROT

USER'S MANUAL BY CHRISTINE PAYNE-TOWLER

© 2022 Noreah/Brownfield Press

ISBN-13: 978-0-9673043-6-6
Published by Noreah/Brownfield Press

Eudes Picard's Tarot © 2022

Senior Editor: Christine Payne-Towler
Content Editor: Jessica Schiek

Book & Cover Design by Dubravka Bencic
Card Deck Coloring by Michael Dowers

Special Thanks to: Casey Duhammel and Michael Dowers;
Muriel Méchin and the Museum of Typography in Tours, France, for
their modern restoration of Picard's Tarot

First Noreah/Brownfield edition: May 2022

www.noreahbrownfield.com

TABLE OF CONTENTS

INTRODUCTION 1
    SUGGESTED READINGS 7
    PIERRE PIOBB'S TAROT CHART 8

THE SPANISH TAROTS 10
    ASTRO-ALPHA-NUMERIC CHART 14
    PICARD AND MAXWELL 16
    RECENT RESPONSES TO THE SPANISH TAROTS 21

THE CARDS THEMSELVES 27
    ABOUT THE MAJOR CARDS 28
        THE MAJOR CARDS 31
    ABOUT THE MINOR CARDS 77
        THE MINOR CARDS 81
            THE SCEPTERS 83
            THE PENCE 113
            THE CUPS 143
            THE SWORDS 173
    ARABIC ESOTERIC ASTRAL RELATIONS
    AMONG THE ROYALS 203

PICARD'S CARDS IN PRACTICE: MODES OF STUDY 205

MAFFEO C. POINSOT'S CONCLUSION 209

INTRODUCTION

When I asked Michael Dowers to color this deck, which first emerged in black and white, the goal was to help make Picard's unique imagery attractive and accessible for a contemporary audience. Without color, these images are a bit primitive and stark. I wanted people to use the pack and experience this groundbreaking Tarot in action, since it marked a fresh start for the art of Tarot when it emerged in 1909. Dowers was not asked to confine his use of color to the conventions found in the Marseille canon, since Picard deliberately broke with that model in his treatment of the suited cards. This is one of the first Tarots to offer naturalistic images on the numbered suit cards, rather than geometrically-arranged suit symbols. I suggest that the Noreah/Brownfield rendering of the Eudes Picard Tarot be viewed as a folk-style personal interpretation of Picard's original sketches, an homage that allows hands-on access to an alternate stream within the Abrahamic esoteric tradition.

This book is intended to make the internal system of the Eudes Picard pack intelligible to those who have found their way to it. I have called out this pack as one of the Spanish exemplars of the Continental Tarots of Europe. This label might seem confusing on the face of it because Picard himself wrote in French, as did Joseph Maxwell who presented the most complete European account of this offshoot from the historical Marseille tradition of Tarots. The reason I label this group Spanish is because:

1) the bulk of these packs was produced by Fournier, in the town of Vittoria, Spain;

2) the correspondences and symbols used on these cards reflect the stamp of esoteric Islam on southern Europe, rather than our more familiar Judeo-Christian overlay.

Interpreting Picard's deck from this angle highlights the multi-cultural influences that dominate Iberian history, during which Christians, Jews, and Moslems managed for significant periods to live together in relative harmony. More research is needed to unpack all the mysteries suspended within the Spanish family of Tarots, but it is hoped that this presentation will help to get the ball rolling.

Playing cards have been popular in Spain since the Mameluk mercenaries introduced them in the late Middle Ages, but it was only at the turn into 1900 that the production of Spanish Tarot decks commences. At this point it seems as if a dam suddenly burst, unleashing a flood of Tarot creativity. As a part of that wave, Eudes Picard produced a print run of 50 black and white copies of his esoteric Tarot sketches, made for the Paris publication of his 1909 book *Manuel Synthétique et Pratique du Tarot*. During Picard's lifetime, only this small printing was produced, after which the carved plates for printing them were lost. These very plates for Picard's Tarot were fortunately rediscovered at a Bordeaux flea market in 2012. From these plates, a second small imprint of 50 copies was produced by Muriel Mechin at the Musée de la Typographie in Tours, and the rest is history!

To synthesize this text for the benefit of future Tarot historians working in the English-speaking world, Picard's original French text has been consulted as well as several public-domain translations in English. It is sincerely hoped that someone will see fit to translate Picard's entire book someday! The particular source we have reproduced here (with edits) is the text found in the book *Encyclopedia of Occult Sciences,* with introduction by (and possibly authored by?) Maffeo C. Poinsot, published 1939 by Tudor Publishing Company in New York.

Importantly, Poinsot's explanatory text includes a chart taken from Pierre Piobb's book *Formulary of High Magic* (which Stuart Kaplan documents was printed in French, 1907). Piobb's chart collates interpretive and symbolic information from a number of decks that were popular and available at the incoming edge of the 20th century. Tarot exponents named in the chart and the article include Eudes Picard, Paul Christian, Papus, Elie Alta (pseudonym of Gervais Bouchet, author of *Le Tarot Egyptien*, 1922), Eliphas Lévi, and Oswald Wirth. For purposes of setting this deck in context, one needs to compare it with at least this short list of Tarot luminaries spread across the 18th and early 19th centuries. The names of more participants in Tarot culture in Picard's time can be found in the final pages of his essay, after completing the 78 cards (p.209).

The system of Astrology on the Major Arcana of the Spanish Tarots takes a modern approach, as we see from the substitution of the three invisible outer planets, Uranus, Neptune, and Pluto, in place of the primordial elements Fire, Water, and Air. In the making of my own Astro-Alpha-Numeric comparison chart of occult Tarots, three variants of (or siblings within) the Spanish family of Tarots have become evident. As you look at my chart p. 14-15, you will see that the Spanish Tarots (on the lowest three rows) represent a three-way discussion between:

1) the model of Pierre Piobb and Eudes Picard (whose correspondences are also found on the *Salvador Dali Tarot* and the *Euskalherria Tarot* by Marixtu Guler and Luis L. Rena.);
2) Joseph Maxwell's book *The Tarot*;
3) the *Balbi Tarot*.

As can be seen, in my chart I am referring especially to Major Arcana systems of astrological correspondence, which have traveled with the Trumps since they first got their numbers. But there is a second internal system that makes Picard's pack unique for his times, and that is his naturalistically decorated Pips, the numbered suit cards. These artistic designs have proved so charismatic that they have been adopted onto multiple subsequent packs, even being spliced onto card packs that weren't originally designed for them (the *Universal Wirth Tarot*).

Picard's cards refer back to the Italian-Piedmontese Tarot of Giusep Ottone, published in Italy in 1736. When we were confused about Piobb's intentions with his sometimes-indistinct lines, we checked with these images. We also turned to the *Spanish Tarot* printed by Fournier in 1975, which is a 20th-century edition of the classical pack by Ottone. These references allowed us to re-establish our visual bearings within Picard's sometimes-surrealistic universe.

In preparing this treatment of Picard's hand-drawn pack, one of our priorities was to retain the full rendering of each card, including his Trump correspondences, his style of drawing the astrological symbols, the idiosyncratic borders, and his unique hand lettering. Having found Picard's grounding in Islamic cosmology, I can confidently declare that the user now has access to the complete canon of astronomical values Picard embedded into his cards. These correspondences have typically gone unremarked in the various borrowings that have been made from this pack. For example, the failure to recognize the Islamic cast of Picard's astrological calligraphy made it seem as if the zodiacal sign of Capricorn was missing from this deck. In fact, Picard's ribbon-like rendering of the Capricorn glyph is emblazoned at the base of the King of Pence's stone throne. Knowing this makes it easier to recognize this symbol when it appears in other locations.

Picard's elemental switch, putting the Water on the Swords cards and Air on the Cups cards, is another clue that we aren't dealing with a typical Marseille-styled pack. Happily, once we understand Picard's intentions, the visuals on the cards bring the core ideas to mind quite well. More examination of the implications of this switch can be found in the AAN essay in the next chapter.

After matching the cards with multiple translations of Picard's text, and also consulting the French original, we believe we have cleared up any lingering ambiguities between the images and the text. In the case of the Chariot card, which shows a misprint in every copy of the explanatory text we could find (attributing the Chariot to Gemini), we have corrected the attribution back to what appears on the face of the card, the sign of Sagittarius. With these clarifications there need be no concerns about the attributions belonging to the individual cards. Whether Picard's followers want to elevate his astrological notations on the Royals and the Pips as a "system" (and some might object that they are not organized well enough to serve in this way), at least we can have some assurance about what he actually meant by his gnomic calligraphy and obscure references.

For those whose appetite is whetted by the idea of a deck embodying mystical Islam, I would strongly recommend acquiring a copy of *An Introduction to Islamic Cosmological Doctrines* by Seyyed Hossein Nasr (Shambhala, 1978). It was not my intention to smother Picard in my own derivations and projections when I started putting this book together. However, once this Islamic connection made itself clear to me, the scales fell from my eyes! Therefore, as you read the text we have assembled for the individual cards, you will find Picard's own explanations, followed by notes from Nasr's masterpiece, completed by remarks from my own experience in using this model through the years.

With Picard's entire pack in hand, students of the Iberian Tarots can gain some grounding in how this pack fits into the overall family of decks. It is hoped that this book can also assist the users of other packs that have emulated Picard's unique set of numbered suit cards. Those packs include *El Gran Tarot Esoterico*, the *Balbi Tarot*, the *Universal Wirth Tarot*, the *Crystal Tarot*, and the *Magdalenic Legacy Tarot*. I have also been known to remark that the *Grand Fez Morrocan Tarot* appears to me to visually represent much of the spirit of the Spanish Tarots, though that perception might reside in the eye of the beholder.

Christine Payne-Towler, January 2022

SUGGESTED READINGS

(FOR FULLER COMPREHENSION OF PICARD'S PACK)

Seyyed Hossein Nasr – *An Introduction to Islamic Cosmological Doctrines*

Titus Burkhardt – *Mystical Astrology According to Ibn 'Aribi*

Idries Shah – *The Sufis*

Charles Obert – *Introduction to Traditional Natal Astrology: A Complete Working Guide for Modern Astrologers*

Marcellin Berthelot – *Essays on Elements*

PIERRE PIOBB'S TAROT CHART

Letters of the Hebrew Alphabet with Pronunciation and English Equivalent			Numerical Value [2]	Usual Meaning [4]
1.	Aleph	A	1	Man
2.	Beth	B	2	The Mouth
3.	Gimel	G (hard)	3	The Taking Hand
4.	Daleth	D	4	The Breast
5.	Ha	H	5	Breath
6.	Vau	O	6	The Eye
7.	Zain	Z	7	The Arrow
8.	Heth	Ch (German)	8	A Field
9.	Teth	T	9	A Roof
10.	Jod	J	10	First Finger
11.	Kaph	K (hard)	20	Closing Hand
12.	Lamed	L	30	Extended Arm
13.	Mem	M	40	Woman [3]
14.	Noun	N	50	A Fruit
15.	Samech	S (hard)	60	The Serpent
16.	Hain	A	70	The Place
17.	Pe	P	80	The Tongue
18.	Tsade	Ts	90	The End
19.	Koph	Q	100	The Ax
20.	Resh	R	200	The Head
21.	Shin	SH	300	The Arrow
22.[1]	Tau	T	400	The Thorax

1. There are 22 major leaves in the Tarot the same number as the letters of the Hebrew Alphabet.

2. Compare this number with the Kabbalistic receipt given previously.

3. This letter M begins all the English and foreign words meaning Mother (Mutter, Mère, etc.).

4. According to Papus.

Correspondence in Tarot	Zodiacal or Planetary Correspondence [2]	Symbolical Correspondence
1. The Magus	The Sun	Will-power
2. The Door of the Temple	The Moon	Science
3. Isis Urania	Earth	Action
4. The Cubic Stone	Jupiter	Fulfillment
5. The Master of the Arcana	Mercury	Inspiration
6. The Two Roads	Virgo	Trial
7. Chariot of Osiris	Sagittarius	Victory
8. Themis	Libra	Balance
9. Veiled Lamp	Neptune	Prudence
10. Sphinx 1	Capricorn	Wealth
11. Lion	Leo	Strength
12. Sacrifice	Uranus	Violent Death
13. Scythe	Saturn	Transformation
14. Human Mind	Aquarius	Initiative
15. The Typhoon	Mars	Fate
16. The Tower Struck by Lightning	Ram	Ruin
17. The Star of the Magi	Venus	Hope
18. Twilight	Cancer	Disappointment
19. Light	Gemini	Happiness
20. The Resurrection	Pisces	Rebirth
21. The Crown	Taurus	Atonement
22. The Crocodile	Scorpio	Reward

1. This moving symbolism of the Sphinx will be noticed: the Iod, the Principle m the great Unknown and also the first finger, the finger which points to Truth.

2. According to Christian. And since we mention the name of the author of the *History of Magic*, let us give his synthesis of the Major Arcana y following them one by one: Human *Will* enlightened by *Science* and shown in *Action* creates *Fulfillment* through a power which it uses according to *Inspiration* (good or bad). Having been victorious over a *Trial* it takes possession by its *Victory* of the work which it has created, and maintaining its *Balance* with *Prudence*, it dominates the oscillations of *Luck*. The Course of Time is measured by *Ruins*; but beyond these ruins we see the light of *Hope* or *Disappointment*. Man aspires to *Happiness*, but this latter is only found beyond the Time and the *Rebirth* following it, which, according to whether he was good or bad, brings him *Reward* and *Atonement*.

THE SPANISH TAROTS

(IN MY AAN CHART)

This text was first written to accompany my Astro-Alpha-Numeric (AAN) chart and is adapted from my book *Foundations of the Esoteric Tradition*, which was revised for this publication. The Spanish Tarots appear in the bottom three rows of the chart, labeled "Spanish Marseille," "Pierre Piobb," and "Balbi." With these decks we are dealing with a 20th-century branch of the Continental lineage that has been uniquely favored with the inter-cultural heritage of the Iberian Peninsula.

As a group, all the cards from Spain seem to be printed with a more striking palette of colors, right back to the earliest woodblock editions. There are many full-card illustrations, and those are quite action-oriented, often displaying the character of one-panel cartoons featuring teaching stories, parables, and myths. Compared to other countries' gaming packs, we see a broad range of races and national costumes, including American natives, black Africans, Persians, and Chinese. These antique gaming packs also seem to be quite free with their esoteric clues and generally more tuned in to the religious and magical implications built into the suits and numbers. Looking at this collection, I get the impression of a lively and imaginative culture that allows for a freer play of philosophical subjects suitable for interpretive use.

One reason for this particular blending of gaming and divinatory genre might be because the production of formal 78-card Tarot packs is largely a 20th-century phenomenon in Spanish publishing. The Spanish cards cataloged in the Fournier Encyclopedia entitled *Playing Cards,* comprising the largest and most complete section of this two-volume encyclopedia, is entirely devoid of Tarot packs published in Spain before the Spanish adaptation of the Etteilla pack, the *Catalan Taroccos*, appears circa 1900. For all intents and purposes, prior to 1900 the playing-card pack doubled as Tarot for Spain and Portugal. This led to Royals that are perfect substitutes for certain Trumps, other Trump subjects appearing on the Pips, and a plethora of ornamental and mythic devices that carry explicit esoteric implications. Beyond the expected heraldric insignia and number-letter combinations, there are lemniscates, figures from sacred geometry, suns and moons, mythical beasts, geomantic sigils, runes, and spirits of various derivations. The visual catalogue of magical and philosophical ideas spread through the many decks in the *Encyclopedia of Playing Cards* draws from (but is not exhausted by) Astrology, Scripture, the Spanish grimoire *Picatrix*, Persian angelology, plus the Greco-Islamic heritage of Hermetic philosophy.

It also seems as if this Spanish family of Tarots contains a higher percentage of female representations in the Major Arcana, with especially suggestive and sympathetic imagery associated with the Devil card. To me these clues imply contact with the most ancient European mysteries, signaling Gnostic, Alexandrian, and

Sufi influences subtly competing with the more Christianized ideas we habitually project upon the cards. These are threads and themes that ride below the surfaces of Picard's cards, despite the fact that this is an unabashedly modern Tarot. If the dates of publication are taken as the dates of creation, then Spanish Variant #1 seems to have originated from Pierre Piobb, (a pseudonym of Comte Vincente). This body of correspondences was first detailed in his book called *Formulaire de Haute-Magie* published in Paris in 1907, just two years prior to Eudes Picard's own book. Piobb's volume is the first printed source for the individual card descriptions given by Poinsot, which we have carried over into this book.

Synchronistically, these are the very same mystery-school structures that Nasr points to as the heritage of Islamic cosmology, although of course Nasr never once mentions or even alludes to Tarot. It is for us to make these transpositions, if such ideas are relevant to us. From Piobb's chart we can see that astrological correspondences are relevant to Picard and the other savants of the Iberian Tarots. Itnterested parties need to at least try to ponder the implicits traveling between the decks making up this Iberic-Islamic orientation. Historians have yet to unpack the implications that a significant group of modern esoteric Tarot savants were cross-pollinating in each other's charts and books across that fertile decade at the onset of the 1900s. It behooves us to try to enter into the conversation amidst them, to find our bearings between them as a group, and to understand these decks in a way that respects their esoteric inspiration.

As we cross-reference our Spanish Tarot proponents with Nasr's accounting of Islamic cosmology, it is important to make this point: We know that Maxwell disavowed any Hebrew alphabet correspondence to the numbering or ordering of the Tarot Trumps. But consulting Nasr shows this denial to be a dissimulation designed to distract lazy students from following the idea any further. This can't actually be factual because the Hebrews write in Arabic letters; it is the same alphabet that the two cultures have shared from antiquity. On page 210-211 of Nasr's volume, we find an alphabet list of 22 number-letters that is ordered exactly like the Hebrew model, including the corresponding decimal numbers complete with Hermetic analysis of the numbers above 10. (Notes on these ideas will be included in the text for the individual Trumps.) In light of this, I would interpret Maxwell's denial as a statement about why his *astrological* correspondences on the Trumps don't always follow the pattern laid down by Sefer Yetzira, which governs astronomical relations in the decks embracing Hebrew interpretations.

ASTRO-ALPHA-NUMERIC CHART

English Letter		A	B	G	D	H	V	Z	Ch
Greek Letter		α	β	γ	δ	ε	ς	ζ	η
Hebrew Letter (Continental use of Hebrew)		א	ב	ג	ד	ה	ו	ז	ח
Arcana Names	Fool	Magus	Priestess	Empress	Emperor	Pope	Lovers	Chariot	Justice
Arcana Number	0	1	2	3	4	5	6	7	8
Gra version SephirYetzirah – From ~1800 B.C. El Gran Tarot Esoterico, Tarot of the Ages		🜁	☾	♂	☉	♈	♉	♊	♋
Old Alexandrian, 600 B.C. – Hermetic Etteilla, Falconnier Tarot		🜁	☾	♀	♃	♈	♉	♊	♋
Continental Tarots ~1880 A.D. Levi, Wirth, Papus		🜁	☾	♀	♃	♈	♉	♊	♋
Marseilles, Spanish Tarot Maxwell's correspondences	Fool △	☉	☾	♀	♃	☿	♐	♂	♎
Pierre Piobb, 1908 A.D. – Spanish Variant #1 Dali, Euskalherria	Fool ♏	☉	☾	Earth (♁)	♃	☿	♍	♐	♎
Balbi, Spanish Variant #2	Fool ♅ ♏	☉	☾	☿	♃	♉	♍	♊	♎

T	I	C	L	M	N	S	Ayn	P	Ts	Qk	R	Sch	Th
θ	ι	κ	λ	μ	ν	ξ	ο	π	φ	ρ	σ	τ	υ
ט	י	כ	ל	מ	נ	ס	ע	פ	צ	ק	ר	ש	ת
Hermit	Wheel	Strength	Hanged Man	Death	Temperance	Devil	Tower	Star	Moon	Sun	Judgement		
9	10	11	12	13	14	15	16	17	18	19	20	21	22
♌	♍	♀	♎	▽	♏	♐	♑	☿	♒	✶	♄	Fool △	World ♃
♌	♍	♂	♎	▽	♏	♐	♑	☿	♒	✶	♄	World △	Fool ☉
♌	♍	♂	♎	▽	♏	♐	♑	☿	♒	✶	♄	Fool △ #0	World ☉ #21
✶	♑	♌	♈	♄	♒	☊	🜁 ☋	♉	♋	♊	♏	World ♍	
♆	♑	♌	♅	♄	♒	♂	♈	♀	♋	♊	✶	World ♉	
♆	♑	♌	✶	♄	♒	♂	♈	♀	♋	♅	♐		World ♇

PICARD AND MAXWELL
(ALPHA & OMEGA OF SPANISH TAROTS)

Of course, the Marseille-style line art takes pride of place when it comes to Tarot traditions in Spain as well as elsewhere. The Spanish Tarot artists never let their minds stray far from that Continental substrate, even despite the Alexandrian veneer that sometimes appears on the cards in imitation of Etteilla. Again I remind the reader that the realm that differentiates the Spanish esoteric Tarots from the rest of the Continental family is the *Astrology* on the Trumps, NOT the letter-numbers, images, and general meanings, which settled into a fairly consistent groove after the Trumps started showing their numbers and the so-called Marseille order was established. Regarding the imagery, titles, and numbers, Maxwell stands within the same footprint as the French exponents, whom he names out as Etteilla, de Gebelin, Saint Martin, d'Olivet, Lévi, and his followers Guaita and Picard. However, Maxwell is not convinced that the Hebrew alphabet is at the core of the Trumps' astronomical order and logic. Instead he takes the stance that "Tarot is a book written in symbols and that these symbols are derived from ideas general in Alexandria, the Graeco-Syrian cults of Asia Minor and the Science of the Universe as taught in the second century AD" (p. 19). This viewpoint leads Maxwell to adopt a syncretistic standard for disposing the Astrology upon the Trumps. IF we take Maxwell to be speaking for the Iberian approach overall, this means that Picard is working from a blended tradition, which is also evidenced by the number of sources Picard collected for the chart he donated to Piobb's Tarot book (reproduced on p. 8-9). But we should not forget that by including the outer planets (Uranus and Neptune at least) into his Tarot Trumps, Picard is planting his flag in the New World of the 20th century, not just repeating tropes he has inherited from the past.

What goes unspoken in Picard's Tarot chart (as found in Piobb) is the seemingly strong influence exerted by the mystical chemist, science historian, and Freemason Pierre-Eugene-Marcellin Berthelot (1827-1907). Reading Berthelot's evocative and illuminating essays on the four Elements while looking at Picard's Minor Arcana cards gives the strong impression that the artist was drawing direct inspiration from this celebrated French philosopher of science. Through other sources I have also found testimony linking Pierre Piobb to the popular and innovative art movement known as surrealism, a trend that formed the basis for colorist Michael Dowers' attraction to Picard's imagery. Once we survey the many cultural threads that seem to be converging in and around the personalities associated with this emergent trend of Iberian esotericism – including but not limited to Arabic Astrology, Islamic Hermetism, the interface between esoteric alchemy and organic chemistry, surrealist art and philosophy, Masonry and Martinism - it seems inevitable that the world is on the verge of discovering a new and largely unstudied world of Tarot.

As mentioned, the Picard-inspired packs have numbered suit

cards (called Pips) which very deliberately do not show human actors, but instead demonstrate various atmospheric and seasonal devices to indicate alchemical changes going on in Nature and in the subtle energies of the Earth. Picard's Pips illustrate the numeric stages moving through the four Elements, and around the Wheel of the Year. His approach to the numbers shows an amazing harmony with the Hermetic 10-stage taxonomy of ideas that Nasr quotes from Aristotle. By graduating his Pips illustrations through these elemental transmutations, Picard offers a profound nonverbal insight into the Islamic stance that Nature is the mirror of the Divine Will. For this reason, I have introduced key words representing Aristotle's scale of values into the text of the individual Pips of the four suits to help explicate the developmental arc of numeric ideas from the Ace to the 10.

A striking feature of the Picard pattern for the Pips is that the suit of Cups symbolizes the Element Air (the realm of the mind) rather than the Element Water. These Tarots relocate the Holy Grail away from the sentimental and emotional life, focusing it in the philosophical sphere, the realm of the mind. Here the crystal cup is a symbol of the soul's consciousness, receptive and open to Divine light and inspiration, experiencing communion with higher planes and higher intelligence. As such it refers to subtle states of meditation and contemplation within an active, aware receptivity to the Divine word. Tarots with this approach often show a preponderance of butterflies, birds, flying insects, and flowers adorning the suit of Cups, sometimes even extending through the whole deck.

Picard's images on the suit of Cups take this suit into a realm that is peculiar to Islam, thus giving another substantial clue to his esoteric orientation. Across the entire suit we see diverse examples of the glassmaking and crystal-cutting arts for which traditional Islamic culture is justifiably famous. The Fatimid rock crystal ceremonial ewers are considered the most valuable objects in Islamic art. Each card in the Cups number sequence features examples from the industry, ranging from "plain but beautiful," through thread trail applications, relief-cutting, carving, mold-blowing, glass painting, guilding, and crystal faceting. To quote Nasr, "...this intertwining of the beauty of the geometry of the crystal and the profusion of the plant, refers constantly to the phenomena of Nature as signs of God to be contemplated by the believers" (p. 6). This is the spirit in which we need to view our Islamic-inflected suit cards with their eloquent and evocative depictions of Nature's moods.

In the Picard-inspired Tarots where the Swords are given to the water signs, the emphasis is subtly changed to reflect the ways we use our minds, our words, imaginings, and beliefs in negative and disturbing ways. The Swords will be shown influencing the currents of the underground river that carries our psychic and soul life, creating turbulence and upsetting emotional harmony. When the card shows the water in a relatively calm aspect, it is because the individual has gotten enough control over distracting and distrustful forces to have neutralized them, or at least put them in perspective. This version of the Swords demonstrates how easily our serenity can be upset when feelings are aroused, how sharply we can react when our sensitive egos take offense. In general, the Sword suit represents the turbulent emotional realm of human society where egos contest out of insecurity and words are used to wound rather than inform.

So although the outer appearances in the situations reflected by the Swords cards may appear the same whether the Swords are attributed to air or water, it becomes clear that the causes, motives, and inner processes will be subtly different as you study the card in the spread. The swords-as-water variation implies that the cause of conflict is rooted in interior psychic and spiritual phenomena; subjective currents are being stirred up as the inner life confronts new revelations from the deep, dark unconscious.

Those who are working with a pack of the Spanish conformation might also want to acquire the two volumes by Harriette and Henry Curtiss entitled *The Key of Destiny* and *The Key to the Universe,* from Newcastle. The astrological correspondences given for the Trumps in the Curtiss books are those of *El Gran Tarot Esoterico*, but the teachings brought forward for the individual cards will be consistent with the times and circles for which both Maxwell and Poinsot were writing.

RECENT RESPONSES TO THE SPANISH TAROTS

In the final quarter of the 20th century, Fournier produced a bright and gemlike restatement of the *Italian-Piedmontese Tarot* of Giusep Ottone originally from 1736. This edition is called the *Spanish Tarot* (1975). Simultaneous with the publication of this deck in Spain, the volume *The Tarot* by Joseph Maxwell (1858–1938) was translated from the French by Ivor Powell and published in Great Britain. In the same year the *Royal Fez Moroccan Tarot* was brought to market after two decades of pre-publication dormancy. I tend to think these events are somehow connected. Shortly thereafter we see the appearance of *Balbi Tarot* (1976), *El Gran Tarot Esoterico* (1977), the *Salvador Dali Tarot* (1984), *Euskalherria* (1990), and most recently, the *Magdalene Legacy Tarot* (Grail Quest Press, 2013). Other Fournier decks that I have found which seem to reflect this Spanish sensibility are the *Marseillaise Tarot* (another exotic coloration of the Marseille line art, 1983), and *Tarot Pumariega* (1989).

It is undeniable that Maxwell's astrological adjustments made a strong impression on the Iberian Tarot designers of the 20th century. Maxwell's eastward-looking divergence from the European Trump correspondences (despite his loyalty to the prototype Marseille-style line art) is what caused me to create a section for these multicultural, orient-inflected Spanish Tarots on my AAN chart. Maxwell's Trump correspondences show constancy with the French Continental Tarots only with the Moon on Trump 2 (The Priestess), Venus on Trump 3 (The Empress), Jupiter on Trump 4 (The Emperor), and Fire on The Fool, #0. These four associations can be considered paradigmatic for esoteric Tarot in every century up to the 20th. Through this reference back to the older Marseille-style correspondences, as well as his loyalty to the look and feel of the traditional packs, Maxwell links the collective body of modern Spanish esoteric Tarots back to the Continental Marseille packs that give coherence and familiarity to the Spanish Major Arcana.

It is also worth noticing that Maxwell's placement of Libra on the Justice icon and Leo on the Strength are standard through the entire body of Spanish-family packs. This treatment of Justice and Strength also ends up informing the packs of both A. E. Waite and Aliester Crowley. We might even see a few traces of Picard's love of the blue lotus (plant ally of spiritual seekers) in Crowley's suit of Cups. It seems obvious from clues like these that the Tarot philosophers of the 20th century were watching each other's work, even outside the boundaries of their own circles and language-base.

All that being said, the most prominent modern deck representing esoteric Spanish Tarot is *El Gran Tarot Esoterico*, which carries a set of Trump correspondences that directly echo a strictly-Hebrew form of the alphabet-letter symbolism detailed in the ancient Sefer Yetzirah. I have used *El Gran Tarot*

Esoterico in the top line of my chart to represent the Hebrew Old Testament canon of magical alphabet usage. In the lines immediately below the uppermost, we see variations that exist within the European practice, reflecting the Greco-Roman reversal of the Sun/Jupiter pair and the Mars/Venus pair. The packs that emulate this body of number-letter and astronomical correspondences are collectively dubbed the Continental Tarots, being of origin in continental Europe and constructed upon the magical matrix of beliefs common to the late Middle Ages cosmogram, shared property of all the Abrahamic religions.

El Gran Tarot Esoterico was commissioned by the Fournier family press in 1977 in honor of the 600th anniversary of the publication of Tarot in Europe. The designer, Marixtu Guler (Marichu Erlanz de Guler), showcases Gichtel's image of Terrestrial Man on Trump 1. This gives us a massive hint about how we are to understand the rest of the pack, for those who have eyes to see. Because the *Esoterico* AAN correspondences match up one-for-one with the Hebrew letters in their natural alphabetical and astrological order, those who aren't comfortable with either the French (Marseille) arrangement or Maxwell's Spanish-inflected attributions might consider adopting this Hebrew model in their use of the cards. (Guler also wrote the excellent and classical divinatory text that Fournier uses for their Spanish Tarot and Marseille packs.)

Balbi's Tarot is an extremely lively Tarot based on the traditional line-art of the Marseille Trumps combined with a set of Picard-style Pips. The unique feature here is that all 78 cards are colored in a scintillating and frankly magical manner. On my chart the *Tarot Balbi* is designated Spanish Variant #2. Meanwhile, Variant #1 includes both the *Salvador Dali Tarot* and another of M. Guler's Tarot decks, this one called the *Tarot de Euskalherria* (which translates as *The Basque Country Tarot*) published in 1991.

What I see among these related bodies of correspondences is that Picard's pack and the *Balbi Tarot* are attempting to connect the outer planets into the Trumps in accordance with new understandings of the Copernican, sun-centered solar system. These new developments forced re-arrangements in the Tarot cosmos, which was eventually explicated, "smoothed out," and circled back towards its Continental cousins by Maxwell in the 1920s.

Again it seems highly coincidental that the *Tarot Balbi* was published in 1976 and the *Salvador Dali Tarot* was created in the mid-1970s, both of which fall right in line with Maxwell's book being reprinted in English and the emergence of *El Gran Tarot Esoterico* in 1977. Coincidentally, these different productions seem to mix-and-match their line art, correspondences, and Pips patterns in different but related ways, making it hard to imagine that they are entirely disconnected. The similarities among them all are a set of Major Arcana that hew to the Marseille line in the line art but participate in a new body of Astrology correspondences readjusting the magical alphabets of the Middle Ages to receive the newly discovered Uranus,

Neptune, and Pluto. Along with this change of focus comes a vibrant body of royal personalities, which often carry an extra dose of mythic cachet.

Appended to those cards is a set of Pips that are geometric, numerical, and elemental like the Marseille-patterned pack but yet are illustrated uniquely on every card. These images reflect the moods and aspects of nature associated with the numbers, allowing the mind of the reader to remain within the Hermetic worldview of the "Alexandrian" mythos attached to these Iberian packs. In both the Major Arcana and the Minor Arcana, the telltale signs of Arabic Hermetism can be found. Picard's inherent base-10 number theology reduces every larger number down to a single digit, while also understanding each single digit as a universe with a geometry all its own. With this in mind, it is safe to assume that the number-letter connections on the Trump subjects provide the links between the charts (Piobb's and my own) and the numbered suit cards.

Also let it be known that all three of these Spanish esoteric Tarots handle the Fool in a way that leaves it un-sequenced, not to be considered part of the 3x7 order of the other Trumps. In my chart the Fool appears in the column that has no designated number-letter correspondence, as would be the case with the oldest decks (although Balbi does give the Fool to Shin). At least some Spanish Tarot experts reject that the Fool card should appear at the head of the number/letter sequence of the Trumps, since they reject the idea that the alphabet is the governor of the

Trump canon of meanings in the first place. The Fool's presence ahead of the Magus card in the Spanish Tarot section of my chart is largely a matter of convenience, because the columns for letters numbered 21 and 22 are taken up with adjustments of number and planet/sign symbolism for the World card.

THE CARDS THEMSELVES

Eudes Picard can justly be called the last of the old-school Tarot teachers. His card meanings are strictly drawn from a tight collection of classical symbol-sets, which are carefully distributed for maximum clarity. Each card is distinguished by its allotment of self-referencing symbols, including the numbers and letters, the title or legend (in the case of the Trumps), the roles or ranks (in the case of the Royals), the position in the sequence of their decimal numbers, the suits/elements, the interior geometry of the single digits, combined with relevant ancient symbols drawn from theology and its related archetypal psychology. As we learn to synthesize the associations designed into the cards through the symbols, we will find it easier and easier to draw meaningful and accurate inferences from this disarmingly simple Tarot.

Here begins the text from *Encyclopedia of Occult Sciences* as quoted from Pierre Piobb's *Formulary of High Magic*, Paris 1907. These remarks are originally sourced from Picard's *Manual Synthétique et Pratique du Taroe*, Paris 1909.

[All notes from Christine Payne-Towler appear in italics within square brackets.]

ABOUT THE MAJOR CARDS
(OR MAJOR ARCANA)

First of all let us say that the whole of these 22 cards refer to the Principles, the Causes, and connect the sidereal world, the Number, the Letter, the evolution of Man. Each is presented under a triple aspect, symbolical, numerical (and alphabetical), and astrological. Number and Letter have their correspondence in the Hebrew/Arabic alphabet, as we have seen. The name of the card gives its symbol; the illustrations of the 22 Trumps show each card's astral character. Let us see what each of these pictures has to say to us. We should add that pictures often vary slightly in detail from one deck to the next. Most Tarot makers grant themselves a modicum of free license in the details as they work through their Tarot visions.

[Here are some overview considerations to help flesh out what the reader will find in the following pages:

1) Islamic use of the 22 letters gives their decimal correlates for esoteric calculations and word/spell formulation. Therefore the numbers above 10 increase by 10 each step up to 100, and the numbers above 100 increase by 100 each step up. This gives two number-scales in the Trumps, one of which is "ordinal" (alphabet-order), and the other of which is decimal. Both Hebrew and Arabic have alternative pronunciations or combinations of certain letters, which flesh out the sequence to 1000, allowing for alphabetic calculation.

2) Hermetic number philosophy operates by the decimal system. Therefore, in the Trump sequenece, we see nine steps "down" from Creator/Magus to the Material World/Hermit. A turn-around happens with the Wheel of Fortune #10, after which the Trumps commence nine steps "up" to the Resurrection (#20, Judgement). In this model, The World and The Fool co-occupy the peak of the Wheel's cycle.

3) Picard suggests various number-letter operations to help the user see patterns within the Trump cards. Additionally, in Nasr's presentation on Islamic cosmology, I found an alphabet list that shows the letters, their decimal numbers, and the standard combinations by which the larger numbers are assembled from the smaller ones. It appears that in Nasr's volume, the mathematical justifications for the numbers 18, 21, and 22 were not included in the account. I have therefore simply followed the pattern that animates the alphabet-decimal-logic seen in the listings we do have. I have not attempted to assign any particular key words to those numbers, but an assiduous student can do more research on Arabic arithmosophy and these nuances will most likely emerge.

4) Arabic astronomy sometimes describes the Signs of the Zodiac as vast towers that stretch from the Earth up into the firmament. This might influence one's sense of the meaning of Trump #16 in a particular situation.]

THE MAJOR CARDS

(OR MAJOR ARCANA)

1. THE JUGGLER
[THE MAGUS]

This is the Questioner. It is Man, a young man, with curly hair, smiling. What seems to be his hat is in reality a halo like a horizontal 8, the sign of universal life. He is standing on the ground where a leaf symbolizes Nature. Before him is a table on which we see three of the symbols of the Tarot: a sword (struggle), pence (gains), a cup (passion). In his hand is the wand of the Magician, of the spiritual conjurer. This hand is raised towards the sky and its nobilities, whereas the other droops towards the earth and its pleasures.

The number characterizing this first card is 1. It is the Principle of Unity. Its letter is the aleph which hieroglyphically represents Man, the Microcosm. Its astrological meaning is the Sun, its psychological meaning Will-power. The Juggler is the man who wants to create, like God, on the plane which is assigned to him. We could with Papus, with Lévi, with Alta and others go more deeply into possible explanations of this picture and others. Every commentator has attempted it. Let us not forget that the Tarot is a marvelous incentive to thought. Everyone therefore has the right to extract his own teaching from each Arcanum, provided he remains within the general and traditional scope. Having said this, we will now more briefly give a sketch of the remaining 21 major cards or Arcana.

[Nasr: A = 1 = Creator.

Understood as Source, First Cause, Fiat.]

2. THE POPESS

The wife of the Questioner, sitting between two columns, a book in her lap, and slightly covered by her veil. A tiara on her head—Juno, Isis, etc. Great Priestess with the attributes of science and the priesthood. Here we have the sanctuary (columns) of the Gnosis, the Kabbala, the Binary. For 2 is the fatidic number of opposition, of duality, the bringer of evil. The letter of the card is the second of the alphabet, the beth, which has as its symbol the mouth, the sacred dwelling of the Word, whence came Teaching, the Law, Occult Knowledge. Number and letter are also the sign of the Moon, the reflection of the Sun as Woman is the reflection of Man. It also reminds of the union of the male and the female, reminds generally of Science.

[Nasr: B = 2 = Intellect.

Lévi emphasizes the Mirror of Reflection in the #2. Ideas of complimentarity and reciprocity prevail. Theologically she's the Wife of God, Her mind provides the matrix of Divine Imagination. In my own thinking, Priestess is the subdominant side of the brain of the reader or querant, while Magus is the dominant side. The two sides need to cooperate in order to accomplish something worthy in the world.]

3. THE EMPRESS

A winged woman enthroned, the orb of the world on the end of her scepter. On her shield is the Eagle, the symbol of the soul and of life. She represents the Ternary, fertility, generation, the mighty balance between active Intellect and absolute Wisdom. Germination, incubation, fermentation, the mystery of attraction.

Number—3, Trinity, Triangle. Letter—ghimel, Vital Mystery, Star—Venus, productive beauty. General meaning—action.

[Nasr: G/J = 3 = Soul.

The planet Venus emphasizes her sexual and empathic qualities, granted by Nature to ensure the next generation.]

4. THE EMPEROR

A bearded Prince seated in profile on a throne, also having an eagle on his shield. His legs are crossed, his head covered with an iron helmet, in his hand the scepter symbolic of generation. Look at him well and you will see that his attitude reproduces the 4 which is the hieroglyph of Jupiter, and the star of the 4th card is in truth Jupiter. This number 4 denotes the universal quaternary (4 elements, etc.). The number of the cube, the emblem of firmness, of solidity. Its letter is the daleth, which means thorax, or better breast, nourishing breast. In short, the general meaning is Fulfillment.

[Nasr: D = 4 = Nature.

In particular what is called the "engine of nature," Nature's vast surging power to grow and multiply against all odds.]

5. THE POPE

The great High priest, the Master of the Arcana, seated between the pillars of Hermes and of Solomon, he makes the esoteric gesture (two fingers raised) and leans on the great cross with three arms. Two lesser ministers are kneeling before him. He denotes and communicates inspiration; besides 5 is the figure of faith, of quintessence, of the pentagram of the Sages of the Nile, of sensory life (the five senses). Letter hé, the breath. Star, Mercury. Meaning, Inspiration.

According to Papus card 5 corresponds to card 2, is its complement, as in fact each card has as complement the card the number of which together with its own makes 7. Thus card 4 corresponds to card 3, card 6 to 1 and reciprocally.

[Nasr: H = 5 = Creator, in relation to what is below.

As I see it, this is how Creator appears and is revealed to the view of creation "here below."]

6. THE LOVER

Here we have our Juggler of No. 1 coming back, beardless, bareheaded, standing at the crossing of two roads. Two women beside him, one wearing a circlet of gold round her forehead, the other with her hair loose. Thus he hesitates between Vice and Virtue, whence the other name of this card, the Two Roads. Above the group Love draws his Bow and hides the sun of Truth.

Now the Hebrew vau represents the Eye, the eye which looks at what the undecided man will do.

Two meanings are attached to Trump 6: Union or Trial. In any case it denotes the antagonism of the forces of good and evil, of Liberty and Necessity, as well as the balance between Heaven and Earth, embraces, love. Planetary sign—Virgo.

[Nasr: W = 6 = Intellect in relation to what is below it.

As I see it, this is how Intellect appears and is revealed to the view of creation "here below."]

7. THE CHARIOT

Cubic car with four columns surmounted by an awning in which is seated a crowned conqueror holding a scepter, and drawn by two sphinxes. Between them on the car appears the Indian lingam surmounted by the ying globe of the Egyptians. Number, 7. Letter, zain, the sound of the whistling of the arrow, reminding of fighting and victory. Zodiacal sign, Saggitarius.

The Victor has conquered the four elements. According to Alta this idea of victory will be seen again in the 7 of Rods which indicates authority in the word, the 7 of Cups being authority in the sentient, the 7 of Swords being authority in life and the 7 of Pence being authority in wealth. In short all the commentators are in complete agreement here. Card 7—Victory.

[Nasr: 7 = Z = Soul in relation to what is below it.

As I see it, this is how the Soul appears and is revealed to the view of creation "here below." Nasr says that the Hermetic scholars considered the number 7 "complete," in that it consists of 3 + 4, the triangle and the square. 7 is also the first of the so-called Noble Numbers.]

8. JUSTICE

Themis with her sword and her balance. Therefore naturally the sidereal sign is Libra. The letter is heth which signifies and symbolizes the fields (elementary labor). This is why Etteilla translated it, visit to the country. But it would be better to say: Continued effort produces balance. And thus we find our normal meaning again. 8 is the number of reactionary balance, of justice.

According to Papus, there is in this second septenary of Arcana, as in the first, a correspondence between cards 7 and 12, 8 and 11, 9 and 10, all adding up to 19.

[Nasr: cH = 8 = Nature in relation to what is below it

As I see it, this is how Nature appears and is revealed to the view of creation "here below."]

9. THE HERMIT

Wrapped in a big cloak. He has his staff to support him, his lantern to give him light. He is the son of the star Neptune, of the number 9 and of the letter teth (roof, that is to say protection, safety). Others give him Leo as his zodiacal sign, Neptune being unknown in antiquity. In any case the meaning is clear: See and be silent. A staff to defend himself. The cloak also gives protection. Here is the true symbol of the Wise man. The unanimous meaning given to the card of the Hermit is Prudence.

[Nasr: T = 9 = Material world having no relation to anything below it.

Nasr is telling us, don't look down! What might be "below" this station doesn't concern the ordinary individual. This is the lowest point of manifestation for the incarnate soul; then the Wheel of Fortune scoops it up and begins the soul's re-ascent. Nasr tells us that 9 is the second Noble Number, representing the number of Spheres around the Earth, comprising the Cosmos. 9 is the first odd square, 3 x 3.]

10. THE WHEEL OF FORTUNE

Iod, the 10th letter of the Jewish alphabet, is the letter of the first finger, the finger of command, hence conception of spiritual duration, then of the eternity of time. Hence the Wheel which ever turns. Here a dog goes up on one side, a monkey comes down the other. At the top a poised sphinx holding the sword in its lion's claws. We are under the sign of Capricorn. It is Life which turns, there is movement in everything. He who rises runs the danger of falling, he who falls has the hope of rising—the fate of all.

With us iod is i, the letter found in the majority of the words relating to water, such as humid, fluid, liquid. Now the 10th hour in China shows the moment when the cows are milked and is represented by an urn, which symbol has been preserved in Hebrew. According to Papus card 10 represents the reflection of the will, the Hindu Karma, necessity, the magic power which is the true wealth. General meaning—Wealth.

[Nasr: I/Y = 10 = in decimal numbers 5 x 2 = the plan of the Creator.

The Wheel of Fortune delivers the consequences of our self-chosen actions. If we have used our will in harmony with Creator, we are rewarded with opportunities that lead to true wealth.]

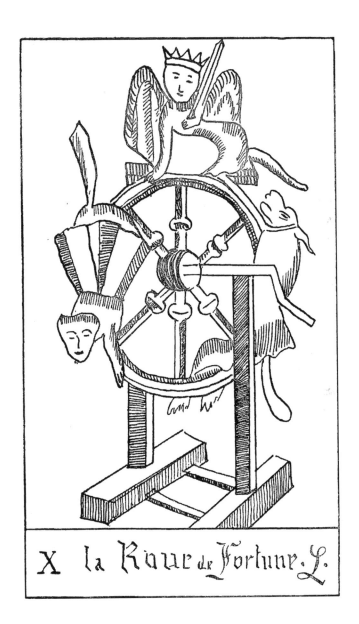

11. STRENGTH

The 11th letter is caph (the hand half closed in the act of taking, of grasping). Hence the idea of strength. Also of vitality. Astrologically—Leo. The picture is a woman crowned, like the Juggler, with the horizontal 8 of vitality. Quietly and without effort she shuts the jaws of a maddened lion. Meaning—Strength.

[Nasr: K = 20 in decimal numbers, 5 x 4 = Structure transmitted to the created realm.

This card represents the courage and will-power required to engage, tame, and influence instinctive forces as they find more refined expression. Notice that 5 controls 4 not only in the Trump number (11 = 5 + 4) but also in the letter K (5 x 4). Humanity (5) dominates Nature (4)]

12. THE HANGED MAN

He is tied by one foot to a gibbet in the shape of a Hebrew tau (a branch between two trees each having six branches cut off), head downwards, hands tied behind him. It represents a violent death, martyrdom, atonement, he who dies for an idea, also public example, discipline. Astral sign—Uranus.

The 12th letter is lamed, symbolized by an arm stretching forth, or a wing, both signs of expansion. The Chaldean lamed on the other hand is translated by discipline.

According to Eli Alta the symbol of the hanged man stands for laws which are inescapable and pass our understanding.

Papus sees in cards 9, 10, 11 and 12 the origin of the occult quaternary, Be silent (Prudence), Will (magic power or wealth), Dare (courage, card 11), Know (the experience of card 12, the Hanged man reminding of the Sun at the summit of its course through the 12 signs of the Zodiac, 6 on each side, and beginning to descend). He sees here the end of the 2nd septenary.

And according to general opinion, Sacrifice is the general meaning of card 12 after which comes the idea of end, of death.

[Nasr: L = 30 in decimal numbers, 5 x 6, = the Divine Commandment.

Nasr shares that 12 is another Noble Number, the first "exceeding" number being 3 x 4, the number of the Constellations. Another concept attaching here is The Sacrifice.]

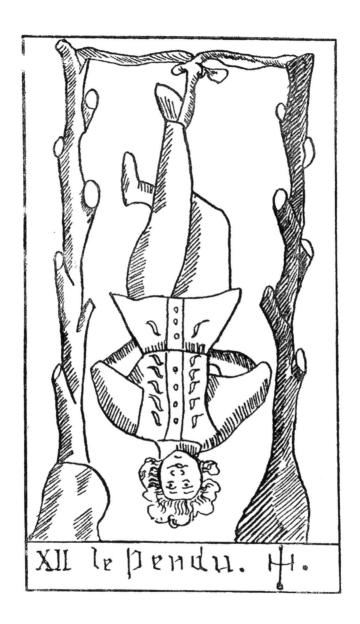

13. DEATH

The traditional representation of the skeleton cutting down heads, hands and feet. Not only, says Alta, does everything die physically, but everything that man does against man also dies. Obviously the number of such a card had to be 13, and its planet Saturn. Papus explains the place of each Arcanum in the sequence by its number. It would be too long to reproduce this explanation here, but by way of example we give his method for the Arcanum of death.

He points out: Arcanum 13 is explained by 10 (Wealth) and 16 (Destruction) in the middle of which it stands (10 + 16 = 26 /2 = 13). 13 is thus between iod the principle of creation and hain the principle of destruction. Hence the idea of universal transforming principle. Further, 13 completes 18 as 5 completes 2 and as 12 completes 7.
And we have the following table (this example shows to what thought the Tarot may lead):

13 Death
14 Temperance
15 The Devil
is completed by 13 + 18 = 31
is completed by 14 + 17 = 31
is completed by 15 + 16 = 31
18 the Moon
17 the Stars
16 Destruction

Thus 13 is placed between the Invisible and the Visible. It is the link of Nature through which all influences act from one world to the other.

Meaning:
1. The Transforming God—the universal transforming principle.
2. The Negation of Fulfillment—Death.
3. The creative astral light. The universal balancing plastic Force.
Finally, the letter mem indicates woman, the companion of man. It is the maternal and female sign personified, the local and plastic sign of the passive image.

[Nasr: M = 40 in decimal numbers, 5 x 8 = The created Universe. Born to die.]

14. TEMPERANCE

The letter noun denotes the seed of the female, the fruit of life, and through this the proceeds of any combination, the result of forces (Papus). The figure 14 is Christ sacrificed, the son of Mary (Alta). Astral sign—Aquarius.

The picture represents an angel with the sign of the sun on his forehead, pouring from one cup into the other the two essences of the elixir of life.

Commentators have seen in this the symbol of the seasons and the changes of life (Eliphas Lévi), the perpetual movement of life, the combination of ideas and forces (Christian), the harmony of mixtures (Papus), the metamorphoses (Bourgeat). General meaning—Initiative.

[Nasr: N = 50 in decimal numbers, 40 + 10 = The twofold aspect of Being.

Visible and invisible as paradigm for all the unbalanced binaries.]

15. THE DEVIL

Picard describes it as the goat of Mendes or the Baphomet of the Temple with its pantheistic attributes.

More simply let us say that the subject of this card is the usual Devil of the cosmogonies, bearded and horned, resembling in some respects the representation of the Juggler. But here the motions of the hands are in the contrary direction. Instead of the Magician's wand the Devil has the lighted torch. The hieroglyph of the letter samech is the serpent (it is the zain or arrow in circular motion) which has always been the symbol of the circle, hence of Fate. This is why the commentators have respected this thought of predestination, major force, evil genius, and have all given to Arcanum 15 the general meaning of Fate.

[Nasr: S = 60 in decimal numbers, 40 + 20 = the two-to-one relation of Creator and Plan.

What you set loose into the world will come back to you. The demiurgic force of the human ego makes everything circle around to itself. Unrefined Mars forces act by instinct.]

16. THE MADHOUSE

It is also called the Tower struck by Lightning, for we see a tower having its upper part carried off by fire, and two persons falling off it.

Number 70. Letter hain. Astral sign, the Ram.

The hain or gnain materializes the vau. It is the Material sense. The figure of one of the two falling victims reproduces in rough outline the letter. It is the first card, observes Papus, where we find a material construction. Symbols, the fall of Adam, the punishment of pride, the failure of the Mind. The balance is upset. General meaning—Ruin.

[Nasr: 'ayn = 70 in decimal numbers = 30 + 40 = The Chain of Being impressed upon the Universe.

The active principle in this image is the lightning, also known as "the finger of God." It can therefore be a sign of Divine Intervention. The sign Aries suggests birth pains.]

17. THE STAR

Nude young woman pouring on the dry soil the vital fluid of two urns, one of gold, the other of silver. On her head shines the Eight-pointed Star surrounded by seven stars. On a tree near by a bird prepares for flight. Hebrew letter phe or pe, Thought, or beth (Mouth), in its wider sense Tongue, hence Word. Here we have the Word in action (pouring out of the fluids) and near by the symbol of the winged soul. This card compensates for good the evil influence of the last-mentioned card—spiritual rising after material downfall. The fault is forgiven. General meaning—Hope.

[Nasr: This category lacks an entry!] P/F = 80 as 30 + 50

30 = Hanged Man, 50 = Temperance. 80 can also be arrived at via 40 = Death + 60 = Devil. This card symbolizes the great joy of the soul when temporary surcease of suffering reminds one of a higher world.]

18. THE MOON

Quite a picture: The Moon in the sky, the falling dew, two dogs howling, two towers, a crab rising from the bottom of the water. A path with drops of blood losing itself towards the horizon.

The Crab denotes the sign of the Zodiac of Cancer, the Moon a night filled with the howlings of the enemies of man and with dread (the bloodstains on the road). Bloody dew, or golden tears shed by Phoebe? The Hebrew tsade represents the end. Hence the towers represent the boundaries, no doubt the boundaries of the human mind. Hence its general meaning—Disappointment.

[Nasr: tS = 90 in decimal numbers = 30 + 40 + 20 = Triple relation between Divine Command, Created Universe, and Structure transmitted to Created Universe.

Using memory and reflection alone, the soul learns to travel by its own lights. The references to blood imply menstruation. Picard didn't supply lines to mark the bloody stains he mentions, so use your imagination.]

19. THE SUN

The star of day sheds its rays on two child friends in a fortified spot. It is the physical father of human beings lighting society, the towns, civilization.

The Hebrew koph denotes the ax, defense, effort, material, existence. Here we have no longer the pale light of Selene, but the brilliant fire of Phoebus. The mind which just now was asleep, frightened, now awakens and seeks happiness.

See how the cards follow each other. The zodiacal sign is obviously Gemini. General meaning—Happiness.

[Nasr: Q = 100 in decimal numbers = 50 + 50 or 60 + 40 = The Assembly of All Things in the Plan of the Creation.

The Gemini twins, representing Humanity, are developing their skills for civilized living in a safe and sacred enclosure. The Sun is our tutor, and all of Nature is our nursemaid. Our task is to evolve and create our way back to Eden.]

20. JUDGEMENT

The dead rise up from their graves at the sound of the trumpet of the Archangel. These dead are a man, a woman and a child—the human ternary. Resch is the head, the sign of motion. Awakening, surprise, and above all Rebirth.

[Nasr: R = 200 = 100 x 2 = The Return of All Things to the One, which is their Principle and Entelechy.

The sign of Pisces symbolizes the last who shall be first. The angel with the trumpet awakens us from our mortal trance, to remember again our origins beyond time. The way is opened for all who can respond.]

21. THE FOOL
&
22. THE WORLD

Some place the one before the other and some write 0 instead of 22. Picard and Etteilla place the World before the Fool, and see in it Kether or the kabbalistic crown between the four elements of a sphinx divided into four parts, and inside the crown Truth holding a magic wand in each hand. Eliphas Lévi sees here the summing up of the whole, the highest degree of initiation; Papus sees success; Picard gives as the general meaning—Reward. Afterwards as card 0 comes the Fool, a tramp carrying in his sack his trifles and his vices; a dog follows and bites him. Meaning—Atonement. Elie Alta makes the Fool card 0-21 and the World card 22 as also does Papus. Of course the pictures are the same as the preceding.

In our opinion this order is more logical. Papus, whom we follow here, calls Arcanum 21 Mate (checkmate) and not the Fool, although he preserves the picture of the fool with torn clothes, going carelessly towards a precipice where a crocodile waits to devour him. It is the picture, he says, of the condition to which we are led by passions which we are unable to rule, the passion of the flesh and its satisfaction, of relative duration, of instinct, the animal sign. The letter shin was the sign of relative duration. On the other hand thau (the breast) is the sign of signs, the sign of perfection. Its proper place is therefore the last card, representing the macrocosm and the microcosm, the whole creation. The four elements of the divided sphinx are:

>Rod—iod—fire—Man.
>Cup—hé—water—Lion.
>Sword—van—earth—Bull.
>Circle or penny—second hé—air—Eagle.
>General meaning according to Papus—Success,
>the Absolute, Fulfillment, Triumph.

According to Picard, the Cups corespond to Air, the Scepter or Rods to Fire, the Swords to Water, the Pence to Earth.

This completes the cycle of the Major Arcana. It opens with the Juggler *[Magus]* and closes on the World, after Man has passed through stages where he develops from his liberty in face of the elements that are at his disposal, until his final reward where he shines in the center of a crown.

*[Nasr informs us of a tradition wherein the Trumps are associated with the primary constellations of the northern heavens. These constellations and their Tarot connections can be found in **Tarot of the Magicians** by Oswald Wirth. Nasr also relates a tradition wherein the expanded Arabic alphabet is correlated to the 28 Mansions of the Moon. 28 is the fourth Noble Number, being the compound of the three previous: 7 + 12 + 9.]*

ABOUT THE MINOR CARDS

(OR MINOR ARCANA)

Remarks by Maffeo Poinsott

We will now pass on to the Minor Arcana. Their key, their connection is known. Each commentator has striven after abstruse explanation. Some are in favor of the Kabbalism of Papus; others prefer the mythological explanation, others again wish to assimilate them with the ordinary playing cards. Alta has his own interpretation, following Etteilla on whom he comments, and Count de Gibelin to some extent laughs at the general fancy. Like a good pupil we have adopted—for after all we must take one side or the other—the method of Eudes Picard, which was recommended at a course of lectures on Hermetism that we attended. Anyone requiring more detail will be able to purchase his book (*Synthetic and Practical Manual of the Taroe*).

In the opinion, then, of the present writer, the major cards represent the Causes, the minor cards the Effects. From the upper plane of the former we pass to the lower plane of the latter, from the Celestial to the Terrestrial.

As is well known, the 56 minor cards are divided into four groups of 14, each group going from 1 to 10 and having four cards representing the human, social, hierarchical element. It may also be said that they are divided into two groups of 28, one straight (Swords and Scepters) the other curved (Cups and Pence), the one active, the other passive.

[Here are some overview considerations to help flesh out what the reader will find in the following pages:

1) Nasr pointed out a categorization from Aristotle, which helps us understand the Hermetic significance attached to the numbers 1 – 10. This is Aristotle's classification of types of words, but it also can be broadened to cover types of ideas. Applied to Tarot, they can suggest an entire taxonomy of description for any situation one might encounter in the manifested Creation. I have briefly adapted the most self-explanatory of these ideas into the individual number/Suit meanings under the label "Aristotle's scale of 10.'" These values could help a reader find customized interpretations for the cards in use.

2) All the knights are shown with their helmets off. I take this in a pacifistic sense, as if to celebrate the end of the Crusades, or the end of war in general. A strong flavor of the Grail Quest and the Troubadour spirit pervades this deck. Picard says about the helmless Knight of Pence "… his reason no longer has a shield."

3) Nasr shows us an esoteric Zodiac that projects the signs upon a mythical compass, linking the Suits/Elements to the Directions and seasons. Rather than unfolding astronomically, this Zodiac clusters all three signs that collectively comprise an Element, connected to a different angle of the compass. The first four signs

*of the Zodiac, representing the initial appearance of the four
Elements, anchor the meanings of the four directions. The next
four signs represent the left-hand (sinister) strategy available to
the Element, and the final four signs represent the right-hand
(dexter) strategy of each Element. The cycle is "read" as if the
querant were standing at the center of the compass, making the
"sinister" sign visible to the left of the compass point, and the
"dexter" sign visible to the right of the compass point. These
four mystical directions represent a spiritual climate wherein
it is "always spring," similar to the myth of Heaven. Notes from
Nasr's spiritual Zodiac are attached to the Royals card by card.
The image can be found directly after Picard's final words (p. 204).]*

THE MINOR CARDS

(OR MINOR ARCANA)

THE SCEPTERS

(OR RODS)

[WANDS]

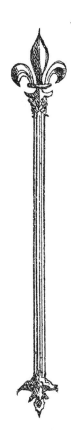

ACE OF SCEPTERS

A hand holds a scepter surmounted with an orb, the whole surrounded by flames. Idea of action, of will, of command. Signifier—Letter, command, edict, decree.

[Aristotle's scale of 10: The substance of Fire.

So mote it be!]

As de Sceptre.

As de Sceptre.

TWO OF SCEPTERS

They are crossed above a moderate fire transforming damp into steam. In the middle of the figure some ears of corn, at the top grapes.
Signfier—Co-operation, alliance of forces for the purpose of production.

[Aristotle's scale of 10: Quantity in the realm of Fire (plural, multiples).

The sun's heat building up in the soil sprouts the seeds and spurs the young plants to grow.]

THREE OF SCEPTERS

They are arranged in a triangle. In the center the caduceus. At the top a dog's head. Around hazelnut trees. All these are attributes of Mercury. Hence:

Signifier—The start of a life devoted to intellectual or commercial activity.

*[Aristotle's scale of 10: **Quality in the realm of Fire (style, shape, nature, innate capacities).***

Literacy, healing abilities, proficiency in studies. Wise guidance by honed inner senses. Confident leadership.]

FOUR OF SCEPTERS

Arranged in a square supported by a lion. Ears of corn in the center. Strength and Fertility.
Signifier—Intellectual fulfillment.

[Aristotle's scale of 10: Contingencies in the realm of Fire (dependent conditions, correlatives; if this, then that.)

Practical skills like farming and wildlife management. Long-term dedication to preserving fertility. Structured progress. The human imprint on Nature.]

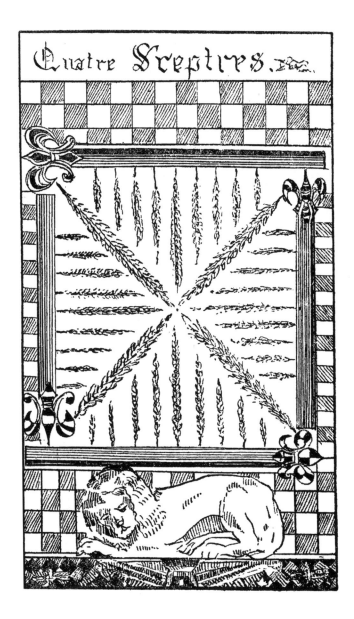

FIVE OF SCEPTERS

Arranged in flaming pentagram (great moral activity).
Signifier—Ambition, irritability.

[Aristotle's scale of 10: Space in the realm of Fire. Placement, locale. Answers the question "where?"

High aspiration and powerful will. The drive to achieve greatness. The "Man of Desire" projecting intent. Impatient with dawdling.]

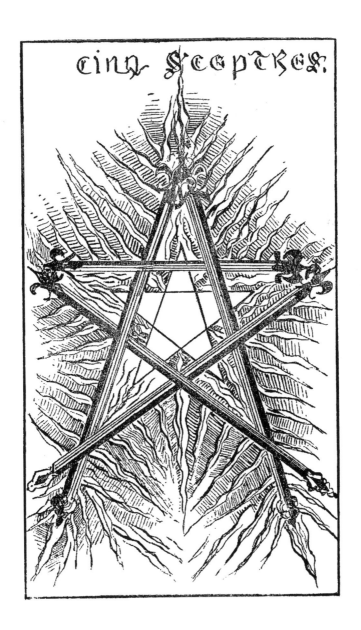

SIX OF SCEPTERS

Arranged in two opposing triangles, one points towards the sky, one towards the earth. Again ears of corn, but their roots are gnawed by ghosts, while on the horizon shines the rising sun. Signifier—Laziness and work alternating.

[Aristotle's scale of 10: Time in the realm of Fire. Pulse or rhythm of life. Answers the question "when?"

One could see the below-ground part as the past, haunted with regrets and setbacks. Alternately the aboveground portion speaks of future potentials ripening under the Sun.]

SEVEN OF SCEPTERS

Four set in a square and three in a triangle above. The four elements within the square. The risen sun within the triangle. Victory of mind over matter.
Signifier—Invention.

[Aristotle's scale of 10: Authority in the realm of Fire. Situation, posture or attitude secure within the results of action.

Intelligence harnesses Nature. Problem solving via permaculture principles.]

EIGHT OF SCEPTERS

They are set in a star; flames at the bottom of the picture, smoke at the top. Balance.
Signifier—Poise. Surroundings favorable to life. The zone of exchanges. Commercial transactions.

[Aristotle's scale of 10: "Having" in the realm of Fire. Possession of requirements, endowed with necessities.

This star is also a compass. It represents the expansion of space and time. Often this card is called "swiftness."]

NINE OF SCEPTERS

Four set in a square below 5 set in pentagram. Within the square a lamp engraved with the sign of fire. Above flames.
Signifiers—Prudence and foresight, experience and lucky speculations, a period of rest from action.

[Aristotle's scale of 10: Action in the realm of Fire. Empowerment.

Personal will rises above instinct and inertia. Plan for challenges and work-arounds as events unfold.]

TEN OF SCEPTERS

Set in a flaming star.

Signifiers—Excessive activity. Work of genius. Harvests and travel.

[Aristotle's scale of 10: Being acted upon in the realm of Fire. Affected by outside energies of a fiery nature.

Like a bonfire that roars until all fuel is consumed, this card represents an extreme state of exertion.]

Dix Sceptres.

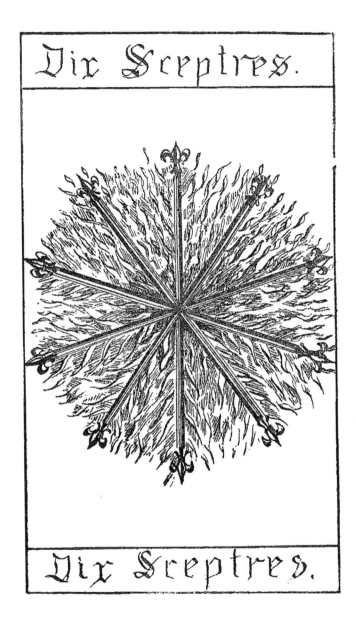

Dix Sceptres.

SQUIRE OF SCEPTERS
[PAGE]

Kneeling down, he plants a scepter into the ground not far away from a wood fire. Sign of dependence and also of youth, as is the case with the other three Squires of the Tarot.

Signifier—Love of home, or youth having subordinate employment with an influential person.

[Esoteric Zodiac: Watcher in the East at Dawn, Servant of Fire.

Pledging allegiance to his region, his season, and the opportunity to advance his station.]

KNIGHT OF SCEPTERS

Galloping in the fire. On the right a ram, the first sign of the triangle of fire. At the bottom a helmet (as in the three other cards of Knights of Cups, Swords, Pence).

Signifiers—Adult and unmarried—artist, actor, writer, stockbroker getting known early.

[Esoteric Zodiac: Aries, Sovereign of Dawn and the Ascendant, identified with Spring Equinox.

Aries setting forth, daring-do, courage, embarking, undertakings.]

QUEEN OF SCEPTERS

She holds a flaming scepter, standing on an arrow (Sagittarius, second sign of fire).

Signifier—Educated active artistic woman, or wife of scientist, artist or business man.

[Esoteric Zodiac: Sagittarius, Dexter Viceroy of the Knight, the right hand of Fire, counsels for creativity.

Inspiring and uplifting personality, brings out the best from each person she interacts with.]

KING OF SCEPTERS

Standing on a lion in the midst of flames, a scepter in his hand, before a railing bearing the attributes of fire.
Signifier—Genius or great talent in all branches of activity.

[Esoteric Zodiac: Leo, Sinister Viceroy of the Knight, left hand of Fire, counsels for Necessity.

Leo, a glorious leader. Autocratic and charismatic. He carries the mandate of heaven.]

THE PENCE

(OR CIRCLES, DENIERS)

[COINS, DISKS]

ACE OF PENCE

A rooted round penny. Elementary correspondence—the Earth. Signifier—Money looked at as representative of matter.

[Aristotle's scale of 10: The substance of Earth.

A seed of pure potential.]

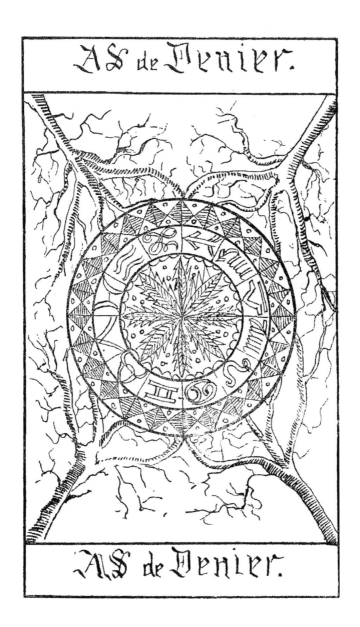

TWO OF PENCE

One rooted in the earth, with the effigies of the Earth and the Moon, the other in the air with the effigy of the Sun. It is the twofold idea of absorption and emancipation by means of gold, the law of exchanges.

Signifier—Contract or business association.

[Aristotle's scale of 10: Quantity in the realm of Earth (plural, more than one).

Giving and taking between upper and lower worlds. Conscious and unconscious forces working together.]

THREE OF PENCE

Two buried in the soil (bearing roots and ghosts) with the double effigy of Capricorn and Taurus. One above under the influence of Mercury, the sign of successful effort.
Signifier—An undertaking beginning to bring profit.

[Aristotle's scale of 10: Quality in the realm of Earth. Style, shape, nature, innate capacities.

The coin above ground is labeled Virgo, which is the sign ruled by Mercury. Virgo is the sign of agriculture.]

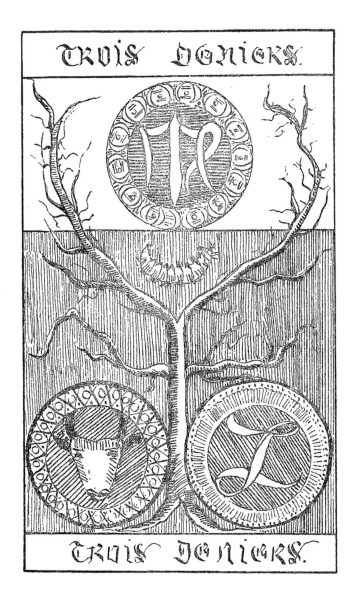

FOUR OF PENCE

Surrounded by roots, in the midst of the picture of the earth. Signifier—Fortune made, daughter to be born, under-ground animals and cryptogamous plants.

[Aristotle's scale of 10: Contingencies in the realm of Earth (dependent conditions, correlatives; if this, then that).

Root-mass increasing. Grounding and stabilizing. Accumulating mass and matter. Substantiation. The coin with the 4 x 6 grid represents the 24 letters of the ancient Greek alphabet, their connection to the ancient Stoicheion (design patterns behind manifested reality), and to the 24 hours in a day/night cycle.]

FIVE OF PENCE

They are round a pentagram and branches intertwined. Five ants are engraved on the pentagram; reason enslaving wealth. Signifier—Economy or avarice.

[Aristotle's scale of 10: Space in the realm of Earth. Placement, locale. Answers the question "where?"

Alchemical gold or fool's gold. Industry accumulates more of itself.]

SIX OF PENCE

Two interlaced triangles with Pence at the points; but half the picture is under-ground, the other above; the first bears the symbols of Capricorn, the second the symbols of the three theological virtues (faith—cross; hope—anchor; charity—heart). Good and Evil in conflict.

Signifier—Avarice and charity alternating. Bad or good use of money.

[Aristotle's scale of 10: Time in the realm of Earth. Pulse or rhythm of life. Answers the question "when?"

Classically, the market maker, moneychanger, auctioneer, or trader.]

SEVEN OF PENCE

Four Pence in a square underground, three in a triangle above; the whole surrounded by a tree which at the top has branches with leaves. The seven planets engraved on the seven circles. Signifier — Charity.

[Aristotle's scale of 10: Authority in the realm of Earth. Situation, posture or attitude secure within the results of action.

The Seven Planetary Governors: In the triangle are the Sun, Moon, and Jupiter. In the square, Mars and Venus, Mercury and Saturn, with Earth in the middle.]

EIGHT OF PENCE

Placed on the eight points of a star, four below ground, four above. Equality.

Signifiers—Fair division of property. Legacy. Girl. Minerals.

[Aristotle's scale of 10: "Having" in the realm of Earth. Possession of requirements, endowed with necessities.

This star is also a compass wheel. The left side mirrors the right.]

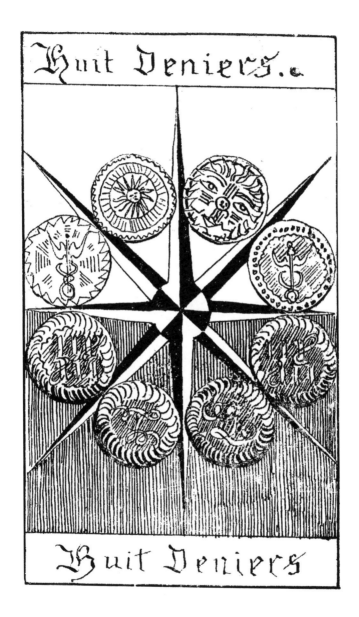

NINE OF PENCE

Four in a square below ground and interlaced with branches. Five in a pentagram in the air surrounded with leaves. Profitable investment of money.
Signifier—Purchase of landed property. Exploitation of mine. Grandmother.

[Aristotle's scale of 10: Action in the realm of Earth. Empowerment.

Abundance, a sustainable system. The creativity and industry of women.]

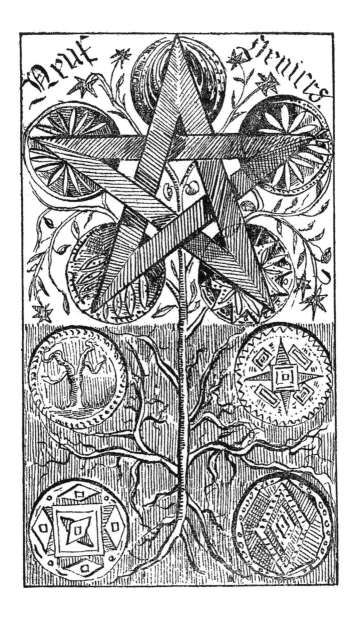

TEN OF PENCE

In a circle, half underground where vegetation is busy. Evolution of matter.
Signifiers—Gains and losses of money, especially by gambling. Gifts. Treasures found.

[Aristotle's scale of 10: Being acted upon in the realm of Earth. Affected by outside energies of an earthy nature.

All the interlocking economies that make up the castle community.]

Dix Deniers.

Dix Deniers.

SQUIRE OF PENCE
[PAGE]

Balanced on a disc rolling between two stiff small trees.
Unjustified ambitions in money matters.
Signifiers—Domestics and thieves.

[Esoteric Zodiac: Watcher in the South at high noon, Servant of Earth.

Small change trickles down to the little people. Looking for a shortcut.]

KNIGHT OF PENCE

He moves bareheaded (his helmet has fallen off) between branches covered with young leaves. Head of Taurus, the first sign of the triangle of the Earth; below this helmets. Ambitious, wanting to possess quickly and much. His helmet has fallen off, and his reason no longer has a shield.

Signifiers—Gamblers, croupiers, fortune hunters, exploiters of women.

[Esoteric Zodiac: Taurus, Sovereign of the South and Midheaven, identified with Summer Solstice.

The quick growth of late spring. Encouraging abundance in the forest, fields, and mines.]

QUEEN OF PENCE

A penny above her. A balcony behind. Woman skillful in getting rich.

Signifier—Courtesan or new-rich.

[Esoteric Zodiac: Virgo, Sinister Viceroy of the Knight, left hand of Earth. She counsels for necessity.

Virgo. An excellent manager, accountant, go-between and networker. Matchmaker. Events planner.]

KING OF PENCE

Is seated on a throne ornamented with two Capricorn heads, at the summit of a rock, a scepter in one hand, a penny in the other. The power of gold which is self-sufficient and has been obtained at the price of desolation.
Signifier—The new-rich.

[Esoteric Zodiac: Capricorn, Dexter Viceroy of the Knight, the right hand of Earth, counsels for creativity.

Capricorn, a captain of industry. New technologies. Backed by the banks, access to precious materials.]

THE CUPS

[CHALICES]

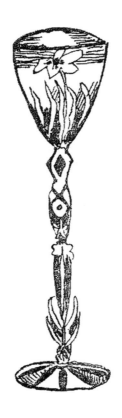

ACE OF CUPS

Cup engraved with the signs of the Air (Gemini, Libra, Aquarius) containing a miniature castle. Above a butterfly flying away. This indicates the house (and the family) moved by confused passions, with the aerial soul flying above.

Signifier—The family, the home.

[Aristotle's scale of 10: The substance of Air.

The work of artifice (the painted crystal cup) is imitating the work of nature (the butterfly). The ideal serves as inspiration for the real.]

TWO OF CUPS

They are in the midst of a crown of roses (the flower of Venus) the symbol of a beneficent binary (sun active in one, moon passive in the other). Tendency to the union of two magnetic principles.

Signifier—Prospect of sentimental union.

[Aristotle's scale of 10: Quantity in the realm of Air (plural, more than one).

Attraction between opposites. Assent. Agreement without contention.]

THREE OF CUPS

Set in triangle with an egg in the middle (shown in germ), a butterfly above and flowers (the awakening of Nature). It is the beginning of the evolution of love.

Signifier—Pregnancy.

[Aristotle's scale of 10: Quality in the realm of Air. Style, shape, nature, innate capacities.

Gestation. Girl becomes Woman. The feminine virtues. Maiden, Mother, Crone. Symbols of the Air signs decorate each cup, but the wavy lines of the Aquarius sign are hidden in the shading. The Air signs also appear in upper corners (Gemini), down the sides (Libra), and across the bottom (Aquarius).]

FOUR OF CUPS

Set quadrilaterally, two vertically, two horizontally. In the center, the eagle breaks the egg. Above—Gemini. At the sides—ears of corn.
Signifier—Birth of male babies or animals (including pets).

[Aristotle's scale of 10: Contingencies in the realm of Air (dependent conditions, correlatives; if this, then that).

Some emulators of this card show the eagle pecking the egg from the outside. However, this text and image suggest that the egg of the Three of Cups becomes the young eagle of the Four of Cups. This card shows the mystical falcon or eagle of Persian mythology, Simorg. His glory and good fortune cover the questioner.]

FIVE OF CUPS

Set on the sides of a pentagram. All around flowers, birds and butterflies. Wisdom and Will-power rule feeling. In the center an owl betokens thought.
Signifier—Renunciation. Discernment.

[Aristotle's scale of 10: Space in the realm of Air. Placement, locale. Answers the question "where?"

Use of the mind to fathom the world of feelings. Objectivity dawning in the midst of subjectivity. The five-pointed star is a classic token of Islamic number symbolism, standing for the individual will and power of agency.]

SIX OF CUPS

Set in two opposing triangles and again with birds, flowers and butterflies. Three cups open upwards, three open downwards. The binary producing the ternary. Reminds of Major Arcanum 6. Hence, indecision in love affair.

Signifier—Scruples, indecision of heart about a marriage.

[Aristotle's scale of 10: Time in the realm of Air. Pulse or rhythm of life. Answers the question "when?"

The busyness of this card both disguises and illuminates Picard's surrealistic outlook. The bird faces arising from the base of the central upright cup are continued below the waterline by the curving stems growing leaves like feathers. Here we see the association of Cups with Air in literal terms. The bird heads also refer back to the Ace of Cups and Queen of Cups. Birds and butterflies above, plants and flowers below. One's thoughts produce an inner climate of busy creativity.]

SEVEN OF CUPS

Four at bottom set in square, three at top set in triangle. Flowers in full bloom.
Signifier—Fortunate solution of material questions interfering with love plans.

[Aristotle's scale of 10: Authority in the realm of Air. Situation, posture or attitude secure within the results of action.

A creative response to challenges. This card celebrates the fact that Nature always finds a way because She makes the rules. Trust the insect pollinators to keep the pollen moving around, and trust the winds to distribute the resulting seeds. Knowledge of Nature's ways brings security and confidence.]

EIGHT OF CUPS

Eight cups consisting of butterflies' wings and set in a star. Balance, the age of reason.
Signifier—Love returned. A boy of seven.

[Aristotle's scale of 10: "Having" in the realm of Air. Possession of requirements, endowed with necessities.

In these upper numbers, the designs on the cups become more distinct. In the 7 and 8 we now see clearly that these are goblets of cut glass. The sharp and geometric patterns are so precise as to break open sunlight and reveal the rainbow hidden within. Notable also is the transparency of these cups when filled with light. Higher reason illuminates the mind. Seeing things clearly, unclouded by doubt or confusion. Eight is the Compass, also the 8 Stations of Prayer around the clock.]

NINE OF CUPS

Four set in a square and five in a pentagram. A butterfly and flowers. Anxiety.

Signifier—Respect for family traditions and principles. Grandfather.

[Aristotle's scale of 10: Action in the realm of Air. Empowerment.

The Nine of Cups is classically a card that implies "your heart's desires fulfilled;" and when the card is upright, this is a fine way to read it. But the idea of "anxiety" is tied in with the frantic scrambling of vines tracing between the cups. Use traditional thinking rather than trying to innovate at this stage. Don't allow your head to get ahead of your heart.]

TEN OF CUPS

Arranged in a circle and separated by flowers. The perfection of sentiment.
Signifier—Friends.

[Aristotle's scale of 10: Being acted upon in the realm of Air. Affected by outside energies of an airy nature.

The cups appear to be separate at their tops but are actually joined at the bases like a stand of quaking aspen. They might also be joined together by a spider's web. This mesh of relationships keeps the community harmonized. This is a symbol of right relationship, the positive effects we can have on each other.]

Dix coupes.

Dix coupes.

SQUIRE OF CUPS
[PAGE]

He is kneeling between two vases of flowers, and turning towards one of them, he smells it. It is the youth of the slave or the first attractions of love. Trouble at the beginning of the connection.

Signifier—Young man tormented by love.

[Esoteric Zodiac: Watcher in the West at sunset, servant of Air.

Awakening to a new motivation. Becoming conscious of others, including the desire to be understood and appreciated. Some learning is required to grasp the rules of the game of love. Imagining the possibilities haunts the mind.]

KNIGHT OF CUPS

He is over a cup decorated with flowers. Above Gemini (first sign of the triangle of Air). Conception of conquest and of victory in love.

Signifier—The seducer.

[Esoteric Zodiac: Gemini, Sovereign of the Dusk and Descendent, identified with fall equinox.

All the knights have cast off their war helmets in this pack of cards. This knight is focused on winning hearts with his courtly wit and noble demeanor. This knight contests for his lady's favor, but he has no patience for faithful waiting. If he can't be with the one he loves, he loves the one he's with.]

QUEEN OF CUPS

She holds a cup out of which flies a butterfly (the soul). Below a cup held by two eagles and in front the sign of Libra (the second of the triangles of Air).
Signifier—The Wife fulfilled, the Mother. Widow.

[Esoteric Zodiac: Libra, Sinister Viceroy of the Knight, left hand of Air, counsels for necessity.

The flames billowing from her cup indicate that this queen carries the holy blood of ancient heroes. Her eagles carry her totemic cup like a sacred censer to purify the air around her. She represents our highest ideals, our most noble sentiments.]

KING OF CUPS

He has a pickax in one hand, in the other a scepter with a butterfly, before him a cup standing on a pedestal from which escape four streamlets of water.

Signifier—Priest, official, judge, widow(er).

[Esoteric Zodiac: Aquarius, Dexter Viceroy for the Knight, right hand of Air, counsels for creativity.

This king is a dowser, his pickax breaks the earth and opens the spring over which the fountain is built. He follows his practiced intuition and listens carefully to the voices of nature. His care for his people and intuitive acuity keep the castle community healthy and fertile.]

THE SWORDS
[EPÉES]

ACE OF SWORDS

A sword which a hand plunges straight into the water where it pierces a crab. In the sky the crescent of the Moon. Elementary correspondence—Water.
Signifier—Struggle.

[Aristotle's scale of 10: The substance of Water.

Sharp thoughts pierce the sentiments. Deep emotions are injured by an excess of rationalism. Thoughts of offense/defense interfere with emotional bonds. What is the purpose of this attack? Why am I doing this?]

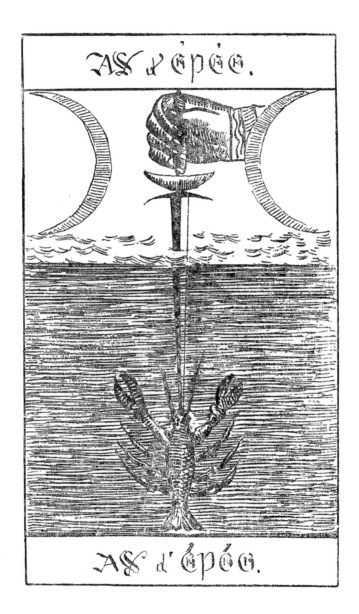

TWO OF SWORDS

Set at angles in opposing directions. The one touches with its point the stormy sky, the other the bottom of a turbulent sea. Antagonism between Water and Fire, between opposing forces. Signifier—Break, duel.

[Aristotle's scale of 10: Quantity in the realm of Water (plural, more than one).

Contradiction. Mind and heart at war. Mixed motives, turbulent inner life. Static released, bolt out of the blue.]

THREE OF SWORDS

Set in triangle in disturbed water. The two swords at the side drive with their points a fish on its back (therefore dead). Three leaves of nenuphar fall into the bottom of the water.
Signifier—Perverted instincts. Morbid condition.

[Aristotle's scale of 10: Quality in the realm of Water. Style, shape, nature, innate capacities.

Consensus fails. Relationships end in strife. Diverging world views undermine discussion. Lotus leaves sink to the murky depths of the pond. Inability to talk things through to a satisfactory conclusion.]

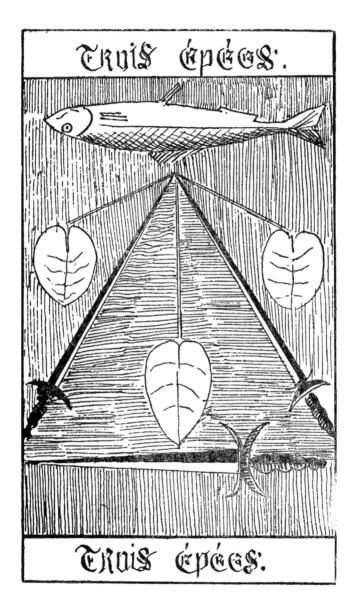

FOUR OF SWORDS

Set in a cross, the points meeting in water surrounded by luminous crescents. Signs of Scorpio round the points, of Cancer at the top. Fulfillment of evil.

Signifier—Ill event (illness or murderous attack).

[Aristotle's scale of 10: Contingencies in the realm of Water (dependent conditions, correlatives; if this, then that).

Negative thinking produces the outcome it fears. Hopes and wishes are not strong enough to defeat mal-intent or repetitive pessimism. The subconscious believes whatever the conscious mind dwells on.]

FIVE OF SWORDS

In a pentagram on a disturbed sea. Above, the eye of God.
Signifier—Remorse, call of conscience.

[Aristotle's scale of 10: Space in the realm of Water. Placement, locale. Answers the question "where?"

Awakening from selfishness, gaining a bigger view. Learning from harsh experiences. Correcting self-centered motives. Insight gained during a struggle.]

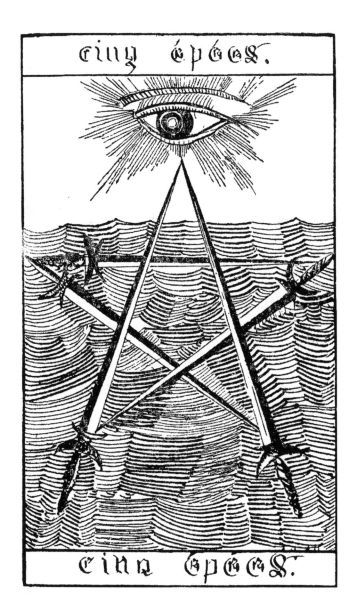

SIX OF SWORDS

Set in two opposing triangles, the point of one in the air, the point of the other under water. In the air two rams' heads; under the water the crab. Struggle between servitude and enfranchisement.

Signifier—Dependence. Doubtful condition of health.

[Aristotle's scale of 10: Time in the realm of Water. Pulse or rhythm of life. Answers the question "when?"

Mixed motives create confusion. Am I leading or am I following? One must decide between going along versus breaking free. There is danger here for the soul that is too trusting. Have a backup plan in case of needing to go forward alone.]

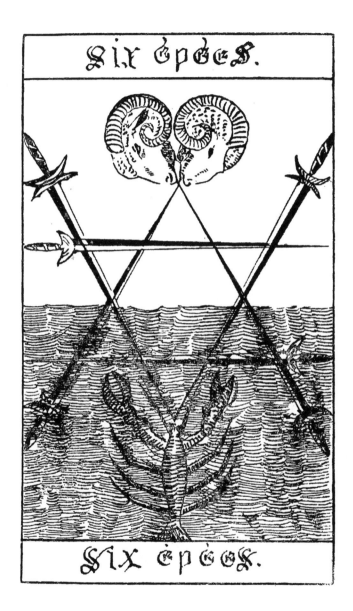

SEVEN OF SWORDS

Four in a square in the water, and three in a triangle, where the cold Moon, the mistress of the night, looks at the submerged Sun. Domination of darkness over light.
Signifier—Theft, betrayal.

[Aristotle's scale of 10: Authority in the realm of Water. Situation, posture or attitude secure within the results of action.

A gleam of light hits a nugget of gold on the bottom of the stream. Is this an illusion, fool's gold? Will the nugget ever show itself again? The light of the Moon is notoriously distorting. Make sure you have more than one source of information and guidance. Victory will have to be snatched from the jaws of defeat. Intuition is required when certainty is lacking.]

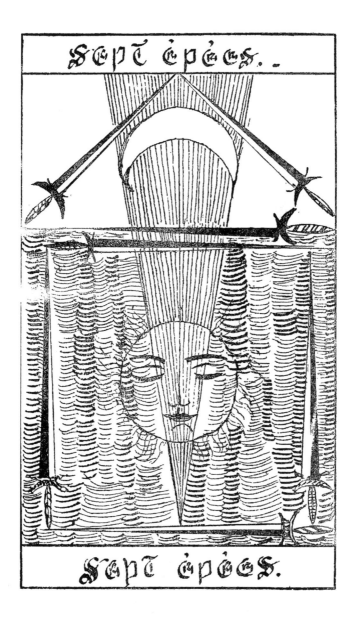

EIGHT OF SWORDS

In a star, two swords being on the water level, three below, three above. Balance.
Signifier—Condemning Justice.

[Aristotle's scale of 10: "Having" in the realm of Water. Possession of requirements, endowed with necessities.

Exacting examination, confrontation with Truth. Being weighed and measured with the same standards one holds over others. No one is above the law. Stop making excuses.]

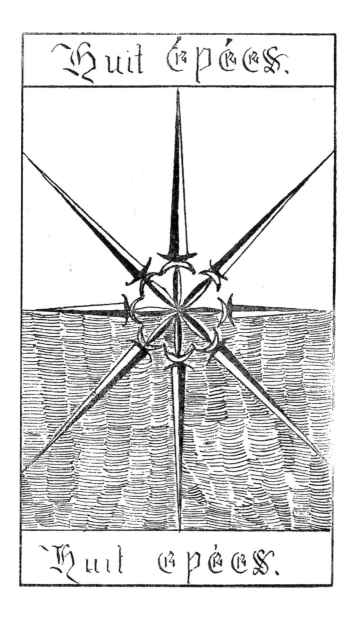

NINE OF SWORDS

Four in a submerged square. Five in pentacle in the air with leaves of nenuphar. Two fishes seem to try to leap out of their element—the attraction of Evil.

Signifier—Hatred, envy, intoxication, decrepitude.

[Aristotle's scale of 10: Action in the realm of Water. Empowerment.

Nothing is working out. The environment is toxic and inhospitable. The struggle overcomes the dream. The leaves of the blue lotus block light from entering the stagnant water. Don't throw good energies into this swamp, they will be corrupted.]

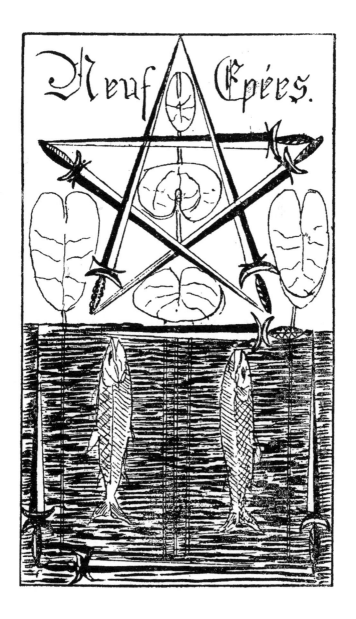

TEN OF SWORDS

In circle, five above the water, five in the water. The Moon in its four phases. This card tells the various forms of Evil and of the menaces of Destiny.

Signifier—Enemies and illnesses.

[Aristotle's scale of 10: Being acted upon in the realm of Water. Affected by outside energies of a watery nature.

The endeavor has ended. Complimentary opposites have lost touch with each other and become enemies. This is the card of "the end of the road." Now that the cycle is complete, the only action possible is decomposition, preparatory to starting over.]

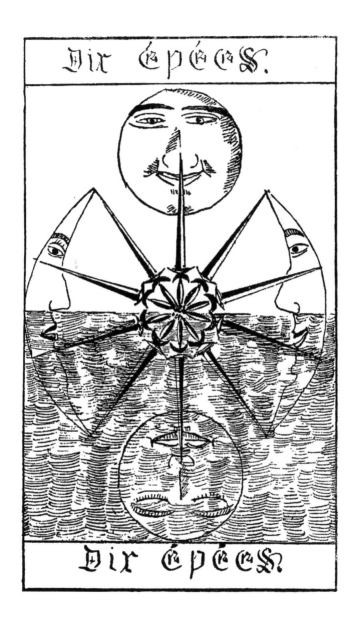

SQUIRE OF SWORDS
[PAGE]

Standing on a checkers board at the water side, spying.
Signifier—Night prowlers and soldiers.

[Esoteric Zodiac: Watcher in the North at midnight, servant of Water.

Spy, intelligence worker. Decoder. Humble in appearance, but very clever. He moves carefully through an environment of high contrasts, carrying messages between enemy camps. Every move is dangerous.]

KNIGHT OF SWORDS

His horse swims in midstream. Helmet and Scorpio above him. Signifiers—Adventurers, fanatics, subordinate chiefs, advocates, officials at the law courts, rebels.

[Esoteric Zodiac: Scorpio, Sinister Viceroy of the Queen, left hand of Water, counsels for necessity.

Danger to those who enter the water in armor! Hidden currents can sweep you away. Know the tides before an attack is planned. Invisible forces can interfere with even the best-laid schemes.]

QUEEN OF SWORDS

Standing on the crescent of the Moon floating on the water. The sign of Cancer in the air. The symbol of the daring woman armed with the sword of struggle.
Signifier—The plotter.

[Esoteric Zodiac: Cancer, Sovereign of the Water, identified with the Nadir and winter solstice.

She knows the strategies of her enemies and stays prepared. Mistress of close combat. She has seen it all and doesn't allow sentiment to distort her aim. She is searching the dreamtime for clues of tomorrow's developments. Her intuition is prodigous.]

KING OF SWORDS

The same position as the Queen on the crescent Moon floating in mid-river. The sword touches two fishes. It's a Jupiterian King. Signifier—Officers, priests, and magistrates.

[Esoteric Zodiac: Pisces, Dexter Viceroy of his Queen, right hand of Water, counsels for creativity.

Pisces. The Fisher King. He holds the wellbeing of his people in his heart. Strong and silent, all of Nature responds to his unspoken intent. You may meet him along the way and never know he is the King. Treat everybody equally, and be respectful always. You are being tested.]

ARABIC ESOTERIC ASTRAL RELATIONS AMONG THE ROYALS

During our material lives carried out on Earth, we exist within the bounds of the compass and the calendar. This was expressed in Islamic cosmology by assigning the four great families of the Elements to the four corners of the day/night cycle. The time of dawn and Spring brings new potentials to light at the Ascendent. The Fire family gathers here with Aries as their leader. The time of high noon and the season of Summer engage Taurus at the crown of the sky. Here the denizens of Earth accomplish their labors with the help of Nature's changing forces. The time of sunset and season of Fall brings the light to its decline in the West. Here under Gemini's watchful eye the Air signs capture the wisdom of experience and prepare the psyche for the coming darkness. Finally, the midnight hour and the Winter Solstice signify our surrender to the interior world of the psychic Water signs in the North, under Cancer's leading. The astrological signs fill these four directions in three clockwise cycles of Fire, Earth, Air, Water: The first four signs (Aries, Taurus, Gemini, Cancer) stand at one of the four angles. The second repetition of the Elements (Leo, Virgo, Libra, Scorpio) has a left-hand or "sinister" relationship to its angle when viewed from a position at the center of the circle. The final repetition of the Elements (Sagittarius, Capricorn, Aquarius, Pisces) completes the right-hand (dexter) portion of their respective angles. This develops the idea of each angle/Element following the model of thesis, antithesis, synthesis.

This illustration is found in *An Introduction to Islamic Cosmological Doctrines* by Seyyed Hossein Nasr (Shambhala, Boulder, CO) p. 156.

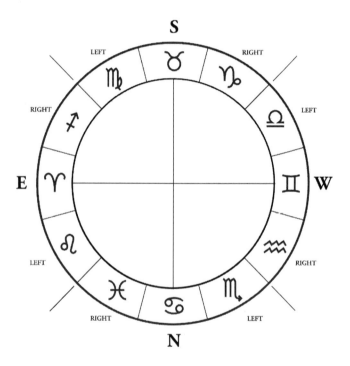

PICARD'S CARDS IN PRACTICE: MODES OF STUDY

*Because Eudes Picard referenced Astrology, elemental theory, and Arabic numerology in his cards, we should feel emboldened to delve into these topics, allowing them to show us deeper meanings as we use his cards. Seek out resources that will enlarge your understanding of these and related topics.

*Shuffle your cards well. Shuffle them at least 10 times before you use them. Let them warm up in your hands. Tarot has 78 cards, meaning it needs more handling than a standard playing card deck to flow and be randomized. Shuffle them freely as you ponder the question you are asking, and use the shuffling ritual to bring yourself to center. Intentionally turn half the pack by 180º at least once during the shuffle so you have different reversed and upright cards in every draw.

*It is best to have a journal where you write your question in clear, unambiguous terms before you lay out the cards. Note down the spread you used and the cards you drew. Don't forget to note the deck you used if you have several choices. I also recommend always checking in on the deck creator's original words and ideas before you embark on your own private interpretations.

*At very minimum, we can emulate design elements that Picard was at pains to feature, using them as the basis for smaller, low-card spreads. For example, all of Picard's twos pair off, the threes can be seen to triangulate, while all of his fours square out on a 90° grid. His fives show the pentagram in various postures, and so on. Each number from 1 to 10 has a characteristic rhythm or shape, which then expresses its qualities through the four Elements. Design small, interlocking spreads using these number-shapes as lenses or mirrors to reflect upon current conditions.

*It would also be natural to lay cards out in a twelve-station zodiacal wheel, following the protocols of the astrological system you already practice (tropical or sidereal, Hindu, Arabic, Western, or any other). Bring everything you know from your astrological studies into the frame of the twelve Houses, which represents the oldest common strata of astrological practice. Arabic astrology prioritizes the Ascendent as the symbol for the querant or native, the person who is asking the question or seeking the reading. Every other location around the circle is understood in relation to the card that falls in the first House. Also, the House position where a card falls will tell you where to look in the outer world to see the literal effects of that card.

*When interpreting a twelve-Houses spread, don't just read it around in a circle and be satisfied with that. Investigate the relationships that appear between positions in the circle. Astrologers classically notice the six pairs of Houses that oppose each other across the horizon (daylight Houses above, dark night Houses below) and/or the meridian (self-oriented on the Ascendant side, other-oriented on the Descendent side). Elemental concords and support structures can be found by triangulating the Houses, connecting every fourth House together in the four great Grand Trines of Fire, Earth, Air, and Water. Interlocking tensions (or tensile strengths) can be found in the squares (or 90° angles) that appear every three signs, one corner per quadrant. Helpful allies can be found in signs that are two stations apart, since they will share the same gender. Aversions and disconnects can be found in the positions one House and five Houses away from the Ascendent, whether moving clockwise or oppositely. Proceeding by this method, you are making an analysis of the question using division of the Wheel by two, three, four, and five to fully unpack the potentials the cards are referring to.

*Illustrate your birthchart with Eudes Picard's pack. Separate the Trumps into Signs and Planets, then lay them around a printout of your birthchart on a surface big enough to let you see it all at once. Lay out the circle of the Signs into the frame of the Houses, taking care to match the first House with your own Ascendant sign. Advance one Sign/card per House, laying the cards counterclockwise around the circle. This will instantly translate your modern birthchart into a classical whole-Sign, equal-House chart. Finally place your Planets with the Signs where they belong, even if doing so "rumples" your modern House system a bit. Now you can see your unique constellations of Signs and Planets in Tarot terms, using this Arabic analysis we find built into Picard's cards. The point is to connect your own internal psycho-spiritual dynamics with Picard's Trumps so that when those cards come up in your personal readings, you will come back to your chart and ponder deeply the reason THIS card came up in THIS position right now.

MAFFEO C. POINSOT'S CONCLUSION

Found at the end of the section entitled "High Magic" in his volume *Encyclopedia of Occult Sciences*

Once in possession of the Key, the Taroc, this formidable Summary of Knowledge and of Fate, may be applied to everything relating to Man, as Papus has shown in his Gipsy Taroc; but we are unable to follow the Magician through his explanations which, as he himself says on the red cover of his book, are only intended for the initiate.

All we will say is that by the aid of the Taroc we first of all find symbolically the threefold theogonic, androgonic and cosmogonic theory of the ancient Magi. M. Charles Barlet has shown how in the major arcana of the Taroc is found the double current of the progressive Materialisation or Involution of the God-Mind, and the progressive redivinisation or evolution of Matter .... which is the basis of Theosophy. F.G. Lacuria in *Harmonies of the Being Expressed in Numbers*, and Wronski in *Apodictics*, have arrived at similar conclusions, namely that all the ancient theogonies are in agreement in their first principles. The Taroc also explains Androgony or the theory of Man who, by analogy, becomes a creator on the Earth (as is taught by the minor arcana), and whose Body comes from the Universe, his Soul from the astral plane, his Mind from God himself.

Finally the Taroc is a Cosmogony and reminds us that the Universe is the result of the participation of the Human in the creative acts of the Divine. Jacob Boehmen and Claude de Saint Martin have thoroughly dealt with this point.

This is not all. The Taroc may also be studied from the astronomic point of view, for in it we find the four seasons, the twelve months (or signs of the Zodiac), the thirty-six decani and the seven planets. Christian, Ely Star, Oswald Wirth have formulated extraordinary astrological theories, the first in his *History of Magic*, the second in his *Mysteries of the Horoscope* of which we have already spoken. Wirth has drawn up a table of the correspondences of the major arcana with the principal constellations of the Zodiac and pentacles too complicated to be dealt with here.

There is the Taroc of initiation with which Ch. Barlet has dealt at length, and which according to him contains the secret of Theosophy, the why and wherefore of the combination of Force and Matter, the union into one whole of Religion, Philosophy, Wisdom, and Science.

There is the Taroc of the Kabbala, dealt with by Etteilla according to the Book of Thot (which is the Egyptian Taroc, also explained by Stanislas de Guaïta, and based on Numbers). And finally there is the Taroc of divination, with the elements of which we have dealt in our chapter of Cartomancy. In these circumstances it is easily understood that the Taroc has excited an intense interest among many. The following is a list of its main students:

- Raymond Lullius (1235-1315), the occultist and alchemist, whose doctrine called the Ars Magna is founded on the use of the Taroc.

- Jerome Cardon (1501-1576), professor of mathematics and of medicine, whose *Treatise on Subtlety* is based on the keys of the Taroc.

- Guillaume Postel (1510-1581): *The Key to Hidden Things*.

- Count de Gebelin (1725-1784): *The Primitive World* (key to the Egyptian Taroc).

- Etteilla (alias Alliette), the renewer of the Taroc pack and of its kabbalistic explanation.

- Claude de Saint Martin, called the Unknown Philosopher (1743- 1803) the disciple of Boehmen and Pasqualis, the founder of the Martinist orders.

- J.A. Vaillant, who spent many long years among the Gipsies and verbally received their traditions which he transcribed in his *Roms*, his *Bible of the Gipsies*, his *Magic Key to Fiction and Fact*.

- Christian, the librarian of the Arsenal. See *The Red Man of the Tuileries* (1854).

- Eliphas Lévi in his *Dogma and Ritual of High Magic* (1861) based on the Taroc.

- Stanislas de Guaïta, the learned Kabbalist: *On the Threshold of Mystery*, *The Serpent of Genesis*.

- And in our own day Peladan, Barlet, Wirth, Ely Star, Blavatsky, Papus, Charles de Sivry, Elie Alta, Eudes Picard, Paul Jagot, etc..

Those who, with the help of these writers, desire to go more deeply into the old Hermetic Wisdom will find in it great profit, and above all an admirable mental exercise. It will easily be understood that we were not able to deal more at length with this supreme and subtle science of Olden Times in this Encyclopedia which only intends to arouse interest and respect for it.

Made in the USA
Columbia, SC
22 July 2022